YOUR SERVICE!

INSIGHTS

'I can't believe the stories you come up with – straight from real life! Thanks for taking the time to write them down, and showing us how to learn from them, too!'
- L.G., Dubai, UAE

'We always look forward to your latest installment of crazy episodes. It's pretty amazing what people do to other people in the name of service.'
- A.K., Washington, USA

'I have been receiving your newsletter over the past few months. I am also reading your book *UP Your Service!* which I find totally inspiring and practical. The majority of it can be put into practice immediately. With results that speak for themselves.'
- P.D., Colombo, Sri Lanka

'I was developing our policy on responding to complaints when your book arrived. We now have a Customer Response Policy we are proud to display. Would you believe I even look forward to our next complaint?! We are building a reputation for great service and *UP Your Service!* has been a vital part of that.'
- G.N., Ski Resort, Australia

'I use your book at my store meetings. My employees enjoy hearing a new customer service situation, and most times I present the scenario and stop short of your suggested solutions, to see what they would do. Then we read what the master recommends! It is a great learning tool.'
- K.N., California, USA

'It's been truly enlightening reading the stories. It helps to "re-adjust" my mindset so it's no longer fixed, but flexible.'
- K.P.T., Japan

'Your "Infinite Absurdity Awards" are hilarious. Keep them coming! But even more valuable is the way you help us avoid making the same mistakes. Keep it up!'
- L.J.K., Singapore

YOUR SERVICE!

INSIGHTS

True Stories of
Winners & Losers
in the Quest for Superior Service

Ron Kaufman

www.RonKaufman.com

Published by Ron Kaufman Pte Ltd. - 10 9 8 7 6 5 4 3 2
UP *Your Service!* is a trademark of Ron Kaufman Pte Ltd.

Page layout by HuiDesign.
Cover photographs by Charlie Lim.
Edited by Brendan Atkins and friends.
Illustrated by 'Einstein', aka Oistein Kristiansen.
Set in Sabon with Helvetica accents. Printed in Singapore.

UP Your Service! INSIGHTS
True stories of winners and losers in the quest for superior service
ISBN 981-04-5939-4   268 pages.

1. Customer Service   2. Marketing and Sales   3. Management
4. Self-improvement   5. Ron Kaufman   6. Title

ATTENTION: Customer Service & Training Managers

Order extra copies of this book at special discounts for in-house training programs, contest awards and conference events. (See pages 244–247 for more video and audio learning systems.)

For more information, contact:

Ron Kaufman Pte Ltd
50 Bayshore Park #31-01, Aquamarine Tower, Singapore 469977
Tel: (+65) 6441-2760   Fax: (+65) 6444-8292
e-mail: Ron@RonKaufman.com
Websites: www.RonKaufman.com & www.UpYourService.com

FOREWORD

What *is* an insight?

It's a fresh look at a familiar situation, a different perspective, perhaps a new awareness. An insight is a chance to appreciate – and duplicate – the good ideas and efforts we see in others.

Insights help us learn, improve and grow. They stimulate new action and make us eager to change for the better.

Of all the insights captured in this book, one inspires me most. Do you know the old saying, 'What goes around, comes around'? I believe it's true.

But I've always wondered who is supposed to start the cycle, take the first step, get the ball rolling forward?

The stories in this book make the answer crystal clear. It's up to me and you. It always has been and always will be. That's a service lesson for a lifetime.

The generosity of your spirit determines the quality of your life. May yours be filled with insights of opportunity and inspiration.

Enjoy the book!

Ron Kaufman
Singapore, 2002

INTRODUCTION

This book began quietly with the first edition of the free monthly newsletter, *The Best of Active Learning*. From two hundred readers in 1997, the list of subscribers has grown steadily to many thousands worldwide. (Get your free subscription at www.RonKaufman.com)

Each month I look inside countries, government agencies, businesses and departments for insights to share with you. I look at people, products, policies and procedures, managers, frontline and back-office staff. I probe the psyche of those who love to serve, and those who just don't bother.

This is a collection of true service stories I have gathered around the world: good and bad, great and horrendous, exceptional, ridiculous and one-of-a-kind. They are testimony to the wonderful people we can be to one another, and the terrible things we do when our systems or fear overrun us.

Many episodes will make you smile and lift your spirits. Others will furrow your brow and make you pause in wonder. From the 'Spirit of Service' to the 'Infinite Absurdity Awards', you'll find them all inside.

I chose to name those deserving of praise while keeping the identity of offenders out of sight. The winners will receive their recognition, the losers know who they are.

If you have a service story to share (and who hasn't) feel free to send it to my attention at Ron@RonKaufman.com

Hopefully the entertainment, education and inspiration within these pages will motivate you to a higher level of concern and care for others. If that happens, then your time, and mine, have been well spent.

HOW TO USE THIS BOOK

This book is easy to study and enjoy. Every story is short – and complete. No need to turn many pages looking for hidden meaning.

The 'Key Learning Points' give you quick summaries and reminders on every page. 'Action Steps' point you towards fast improvement and easy implementation of the best ideas.

This book is also easy to share with others. Show a chapter to your boss if she doesn't understand. Pick a story for your staff when they need a service boost. Give a copy to your partners, colleagues and suppliers so they can meet, then exceed, your expectations.

As you read, you'll notice more about the service that surrounds you: in your home, school, community, government and business interactions. When you see good service, use the ideas in this book to praise it. When you get lousy treatment, share the lessons in this book to help them serve you better.

If you are in business, this book can help you create truly loyal customers – happy clients who come back, buy more and tell their friends about you.

If you are building a culture of excellent service, take heart! It's not a mystery or magical science. Great service cultures are the result of deliberate effort, genuine passion, in-depth service knowledge and continuous commitment to improve. This book will help you gain them all.

But not everyone is ready to make such an effort, maintain such a focus and take the necessary actions. Are you?

CONTENTS

FOREWORD   VII

INTRODUCTION   IX

HOW TO USE THIS BOOK   XI

CONTENTS   XII-XIX

CHAPTER 1

Service is an Inside Job   **1**

Stretching your sense of service   2

100% is not enough. You need 120%!   3

Get yourself spring-loaded   4

The motivating power of purpose   5

You have leverage. Use it.   6

Leave this place better than you found it   7

The amazing Harvey Mackay   8-9

Personal Diamond Awards   10-11

Lost the fire? Time to retire!   12-13

Serving others? Serve yourself!   14

Give the gift of giving   15

CHAPTER 2

The Heart of the Matter   **17**

In the spirit of service   18

In customers we trust   19

Moment of truth or moment of impact?   20

Helping others succeed is good service   21

Create your own 'Godiva moment'	22-23
Find and do your own thing	24-25
Say the magic words	26-27
Turning provocation into pleasure	28-29
You may never know what's really going on	30-31
What to do when your customer is about to explode	32-33
As much as possible, forgive them	34-35
Handling customer abuse	36
To inspire perfect service – tip!	37
Nice work! Well done! Keep it up!	38

CHAPTER 3

The Spirit of the Team — **39**

One shared voice to the customer	40-41
'A' is for outstanding	42-43
Feedback is the breakfast of champions	44
Four questions to boost collaboration	45
Co-pay is a win–win–win	46-47
Get out of the Ivory Tower	48
Keeping in touch at Popeye's	49
Future sales are hiding in service	50-51
Service begins in sales, new sales begin in service	52-53
Winning and losing in the pit stop	54
Literally 'burying the hatchet'	55

CHAPTER 4

Listen to the Language — **57**

Will this settle the case?	58-59
Well then, who do you do it for?	60

Is the customer really king?   61
It's a lose–lose–lose situation   62
Keeping high tech, high touch   63
Unsuccessful applicants deserve good
service too   64
The power of a pregnant pause   65
Who loves the taxman?   66-67
An apple a day keeps the customer   68
Pick the words with power   69
Standing out in the crowd   70
A promise to remember   71
Satisfaction plus for a better world   72-73
Australian service gets hopping   74-75
You get a little more when you come
to Singapore   76

CHAPTER 5

Generating New Ideas   **77**

Is consensus sinking your organization?   78-79
The playful policy review   80-81
Put some stuffing in the staff
suggestion box   82-83
If we implement them all, you have
not succeeded   84
Push into the white space   85
Whine, moan and complain – then
contribute!   86-87
We have a responsibility to the future   88

CHAPTER 6

Positive, Productive Partners   **89**

Creating partnership agreements   90
Cross-town collaboration   91

Are you pulling in the same direction?   92-93

Do 'captive customers' deserve
great service?   94-95

Keep your suppliers eager with a
70/30 split   96

You're as good as your weakest link   97

CHAPTER 7

Creating Service Culture   **99**

Four steps to a better service culture   100

Stop looking for the 'X factor'   101

Eye-to-eye at the 'Staff Recognition Center'   102

Chasing chickens builds a better culture   103

How *hot* is our service?   104-105

The 'friendliest airport in the world'   106

Driving home the culture of honesty   107

The Police Debates   108-109

A rising tide lifts all boats – except
those that sink!   110

No news is…bad news!   111

Complaints + compliments = good
communication   112-113

8 ways to get close to your customer   114-115

Develop a yearning for learning   116-117

CHAPTER 8

Personal and Proactive   **119**

Positive, proactive communication   120-121

Make it person-to-person   122-123

To build your business, appreciate
the customers you already have   124-125

How to pay a powerful compliment   126-127

Flexibility slakes a thirst   128

Peach pie with your scuba-dive? 129

If not this time, perhaps later 130

The other guy has a better deal 131

Meet Elvis, King of the Road 132

CHAPTER 9

Setting the Pace, Leading the Race **133**

What is 'Legendary Service'? 134-135

Federal Express sets a benchmark 136-137

Education is the star at Starbucks 138-139

My new hat makes me information rich! 140

Innovation magnifies your service 141

IKEA turns common sense upside down 142

Ireland's 'express lane' makes sense 143

It's not about the price... 144

Million-dollar voice mail 145

Palm Pilot wins with positive word-of-mouth 146

Little things can mean a lot 147

Only 'Top Box Quality' at Motorola 148

CHAPTER 10

Building Up Your Business **149**

1:1 – The next wave in customer care 150-151

Credibility comes from the customer 152-153

How much service is *too much* service? 154-155

Customer satisfaction is a rearview mirror 156

Twenty words to build a better future 157

The customer's tastebuds are always right 158

The positive power of competition 159

Add value first, *reap* value later 160

Give a gift that gives again 161

Beta means never having to say you're sorry 162

Give yourself a vigorous visual audit   163
Give yourself an auditory audit   164-165
Customer loyalty – in the hospital?   166-167
What is Ron's website really for?   168-169

CHAPTER 11
When Things Go Wrong   **171**

Don't be a softie...*squeak*!   172-173
How to put loyalty at risk   174-175
Who were they designing it for?   176-177
Why is this information hidden?   178
Who put sand in the grease?   179
How to *lose* a customer for life   180-181
An upgrade is usually worse, at first   182

CHAPTER 12
Service Recovery = Customer Loyalty   **183**

It was an accident! (Now what do
you do?)   184-185
Total recovery = customer delight   186-187
1,500 puzzle pieces...minus one!   188
Laundry Unlimited 'bounces back'   189
Preserve the loyalty you deserve   190-191
Managing customer complaints   192-193
Track each complaint until your
customer comes back   194

CHAPTER 13
The Infinite Absurdity Awards   **195**

Don't let your systems drive your
customers crazy!   196-197
The conference rate in Los Angeles   198-199

Hertz Rent-a-Car in San Francisco 200-201
You can't have juice with a Special
Broiler Meal 202-203
Doing right – or doing better? 204-205
Getting (dis)connected 206-207
Your goodwill has expired 208
We are really sorry for you, but... 209
But everybody knows about it 210-211
Never on a sundae 212-213
Developing an eye for detail 214-215
Lack of integration = customer
frustration 216-217
Please drive around once again 218

CHAPTER 14

Sometimes Service Stinks   **219**

The cheesecake of tomorrow 220
Yes, we have no bananas 221
For just 30 cents of salad... 222-223
The holidays are here 224
A hard taste from a soft drink 225
Customer recovery first, system
recovery second! 226
Where on the floor is 264? 227
Customers...NO! 228
How to be customer unfriendly 229
Are you referable? 230
Turtles deliver the internal mail 231
Who's answering your e-mail? 232
How not to build with bytes 233

CHAPTER 15
Final Thoughts 235

What level of service do you provide?   236-239
Have you learned to savor the victory?   240
'Perfect lives'   241
More...is more than enough   242

UP Your Service! learning resources   244-247

I

SERVICE IS AN INSIDE JOB

'Ahh... The secret of superior
service is deep within you.'

Stretching your sense of service

How far does your service go? And how much farther can you stretch it?

If you serve customers, do you stretch to do it better every day? Are you eager to learn from colleagues and mentors, seminars, books, websites...and a healthy dose of candid customer feedback?

If you provide internal service, do you reach across functional lines, or stay stuck inside your departmental 'silo'? Is your communication with colleagues and partners positive, proactive and persistent?

If you serve in your community, do you volunteer time and stretch a little more by asking others to join you?

If you serve your family, do you reach out with a higher level of attention and affection every day?

If you serve the planet, are you ecologically aware? Do your actions inspire and educate the neighbors?

If you serve humanity, do you cultivate true compassion, patience, kindness, respect and encouragement of others?

If you serve all life, have you expanded your sense of life itself and your understanding of what it means, being here 'in service'?

Key Learning Point

Service is a great line of work, and those of us who do it daily are certainly among the fortunate on Earth. You can increase your good fortune, and that of others, by deepening your commitment and expanding the impact of your service every day.

Action Steps

Make an extra effort to s-t-r-e-t-c-h your sense of service. Each day, offer a little more than you did yesterday.

100% is not enough. You need 120%!

I recently organized a service benchmarking visit to Singapore for 22 Korean sales and service trainers. In seven days we visited 23 leading organizations. A very busy week!

At the Singapore Airlines Cabin Crew Training Centre, one visitor asked, 'How does Singapore Airlines stay on top all these years? And how do you plan to keep the lead while other airlines work so hard to beat you?'

Senior Vice President, Mr Sim Kay Wee, answered clearly: '100% is not enough. When you reach #1, you need 120%.

'Here's why: If you fly on a mediocre airline, your service expectation may be only 50%. If the cabin crew is in a better mood, they may actually deliver 65%. Then what is your opinion of the service? It's up 15%!

'Now if you know Singapore Airlines is #1, what is your expectation of the service? 110%! And if our cabin crew delivers service only at the 100% level, what is your opinion of the service? It's down 10%!

'This is the challenge of being #1,' he concluded. 'If you are in the lead and want to stay there, 100% is not enough. You need every member of the team to give 120%!'

Key Learning Point

If you work hard and smart you may finally reach the top – #1! And then what? If you want to stay there, you've got to work even harder, and smarter! Give it your all. Give it your best. Give it 120%.

Action Steps

Take your best past performance as 100%. What would a 120% service effort look like? 120% results? Make that your team target for today.

Get yourself spring-loaded

An e-mail arrived with a fragmentary phrase that absolutely caught my attention. The writer referred to many upset customers being 'spring-loaded in the pissed-off position'.

What a phrase! And what an observation.

Ever noticed how quickly *you* get triggered when the service you receive goes bad? Ever noticed how short the fuse can be on the customers around you?

I decided to try the *opposite* approach and see what happens. I've been traveling a lot lately, and whenever I've needed personal service, I put myself in an intentionally good mood: 'spring-loaded in the appreciative position'.

Guess what happened?

I met friendly waiters, chatty taxi drivers and airline check-in agents who went out of their way to help me. I got telephone assistance way beyond expectations and found sales staff who were polite and eager to please. Everywhere I turned, service providers gladly went above and beyond the normal call of duty.

I wonder why? Was it something in the water? Something in the air? Or something more fundamental – about me?

Key Learning Point

Service is a two-way street. Life is, too. Want good service? What you send out comes right back to you.

Action Steps

Make the decision to get great service from today. It's easy! Just get yourself 'spring-loaded in the appreciative position'.

The motivating power of purpose

Patrick Atkins is Senior Manager for Agency Training of a major insurance company. When people asked what he did for a living, he used to reply, 'I sell life insurance'.

In his second year of selling, a customer died in an accident and he went to visit the widow. She was distraught, of course, but she spoke to Patrick after the funeral.

'I always resented the money my husband spent on insurance,' she said. 'I thought it was wasted money that we could have used for something else. But now your insurance payment is going to allow my children to stay in school and give us enough money to keep living in this house. You've saved our family.'

Today, when people ask Patrick Atkins what he does for a living, he says with sincerity and pride, 'I save families'.

Patrick Atkins saves families for a living. What about you? What do you do that helps people enjoy, grow and live a better life? What's the motivating power in your purpose?

Key Learning Point

Providing great service to others can be hard work. Your customers may be upset, demanding, problematic – even mean. You need an uplifting purpose to keep you going, bring you up when times are hard and inspire you to keep on serving.

Action Steps

Clarify what you do and how it helps other people live a better life. Then, the next time someone asks what you do for a living, give them the *real* answer.

You have leverage. Use it.

I spoke to 1,200 police officers about delivering security and high quality service.

One officer asked: 'In this city there are 3,000 police and more than 3,000,000 members of the public. What difference can we few possibly make to improve service throughout this country?'

I replied, 'You have leverage. Use it.'

Imagine you are sitting at an outdoor restaurant in a busy part of town. Hundreds of tourists, shoppers and business people are walking along. A police officer in uniform strolls by. Would you notice him right away? Of course.

Now suppose the officer detours and walks towards a soda can or empty coffee cup someone left on the ground. He picks it up, takes a few steps and deposits the litter in a trash bin. Would you notice what he did? Of course.

How would you feel at that moment, about the litter, and the police? Would you ridicule the officer in your mind? Or would you notice his effort, appreciate his action, and feel good about him making the city just a little cleaner?

In the following hours and days, would you litter or leave your trash behind? Not likely.

Key Learning Point

Where do you have 'leverage' in your life? Where is your reputation held up high? At your work, in your community, in your neighborhood or home? Wherever it may be, use your leverage to everyone's advantage.

Action Steps

Be *seen* to make a difference. Take the constructive action that will be noticed and appreciated by all. Take positive actions that no one notices, too. Because *you* will notice, and that's powerful leverage with yourself.

Leave this place better than you found it

I stepped into the restroom of a large office building before a meeting. The paper towel dispenser had come unhinged and fresh towels were scattered on the floor. Many were wet and had been stepped on by those who came before me.

Despite being in my suit and tie, I bent down to pick up the remaining dry towels and placed them near the sink. I gathered the wet and dirty towels and put them in the trash. Then I found the receptionist and asked her to inform Maintenance about the broken dispenser inside.

As I was cleaning up, several people entered the restroom. I wondered what they thought of me, picking up wet and dirty paper towels in my suit and tie? Did they think I broke the dispenser? Did they think I worked in the building?

Then I realized how I felt about myself. I felt good doing more than 'what's expected'. My contribution was very small, but it made the restroom a better place for everyone.

Key Learning Point

We are all beneficiaries of public spaces: parks, roads, buildings, restaurants, shopping malls and parking lots. Instead of being just another user of these conveniences, be an active partner in their upkeep, maintenance and care. It's not what others think of you that counts, it's what you think about yourself.

Action Steps

Light burned out? Tell someone it needs changing. A leak along the floor? Report it with a phone call. Toilet paper running low? Be the one to tell the staff. See that litter in the park? Pick it up and toss it out. Did the people before you at a fast-food restaurant forget to clear their tray? Clear the table for them. What the heck, clear two!

The amazing Harvey Mackay

Harvey Mackay is the author of *Swim With the Sharks Without Being Eaten Alive* and other bestsellers. More than 10,000,000 of his books have been purchased around the world.

Harvey is founder of the Mackay Envelope Corporation and is one remarkable human being. I had the pleasure of sharing a speaker's platform with him at an Achiever's Congress in Asia.

Harvey says the 'real title' of all his popular business books is *Prepare to Win* – get yourself ready to succeed through vigorous and early preparation.

He demonstrated this masterfully in the way he prepared for his upcoming speech in Asia. One month before the program, Harvey spent two hours with me on the telephone from his office in the United States. He wanted to know everything about the local audience: social trends, history, culture, economy, politics, races, religion, concerns, aspirations, hopes, fears and more.

When he got off the plane in Asia, Harvey's research and preparation continued. He asked everyone he met for their personal insights on important issues of the day. By constantly asking and carefully listening, Harvey prepared himself (and his audience) to win.

He pored through the local papers and studied radio and television programs. He listened carefully to every speaker who preceded him on the platform.

And when Harvey Mackay walked on stage to deliver his 90-minute presentation, he had more customized notes sticking to the pages of his speech than I have seen anyone carry in years!

All his preparation paid off. Harvey's integration of every idea, example and illustration was seamless. No one knew how many hours he had spent adjusting, improving and fine-tuning his speech for just this particular audience.

No one, that is, except Harvey Mackay.

Key Learning Point

Harvey's original mission statement for the Mackay Envelope Corporation was: *'To be in business forever'*. His passion for preparation is one way Harvey works to achieve this goal.

What if this was your mission statement?

How would you change your approach? How much time and effort would you invest to prepare, serve and delight your customers, partners and staff?

Learn from Harvey Mackay. Try it today.

Action Steps

Harvey Mackay's five rules for success in presentations – and in life:

1. Show up. (80% success)

2. Show up on time. (85% success)

3. Show up on time with a plan. (90% success)

4. Show up on time with a plan committed to excellence. (95% success)

5. Show up on time with a plan committed to excellence and then execute. (100% success)

For much more of Harvey Mackay's insight and practical wisdom, visit www.mackay.com

Personal Diamond Awards

The Olympic Games are a global celebration of challenge, performance and achievement. Around the world, viewers thrill to see who takes home the Bronze, Silver and Gold.

I enjoy looking deeper, silently granting 'Personal Diamond Awards' to anyone who goes faster, higher or longer and achieves a 'personal best'.

What would the Olympics be like if we officially included the Personal Diamond Awards?

Imagine an athlete who wins the bronze medal as well as a Personal Diamond. How would that athlete react? How might the audience respond? Would the bronze medalist begrudge the silver or gold medal winners? Not at all. Would the silver and gold winners offer their sincere and heartfelt congratulations? Absolutely.

Imagine an athlete who wins no medal at all, yet still achieves a Personal Diamond. Would he go home beaten and dismayed? Or elated by his achievement? Would his compatriots be disappointed or encouraged?

Imagine an athlete who wins the gold medal with a Personal Diamond performance. How would the audience and athletes respond to that record-setting personal *and* global achievement?

Now think about your family, your company and your department. How might life around you be enhanced by granting Personal Diamond Awards?

Would others be inspired by recognition of their 'personal best' in service, sales, teamwork, speed or innovation? Would they be more willing, more engaging, or more helpful and encouraging towards others?

Now think about yourself. What personal bests are you aiming to reach today? Is it focus, attention, commitment, generosity, forgiveness, responsibility or relaxation?

How would you feel about a Personal Diamond Award extended from those who know you well? How would you feel about a Personal Diamond that you recognize and award to yourself?

Key Learning Point

We perform in the Olympics of our lives every day. Whatever the field of your endeavor or the circumstances you face, your life deserves your very best.

Action Steps

The next time someone achieves a personal best, acknowledge them with a Personal Diamond Award. They will feel stronger and more committed. You'll feel terrific, too.

Lost the fire? Time to retire!

I was flying to the United States when an In-Flight Supervisor recognized me and came over to chat. We spoke about current challenges and how quickly the airline was growing.

She lamented that some older crew felt jaded and uninspired. They tend to do the minimum of work in flight, she said, shifting the burden to younger crew members. This behavior was setting a poor example and had a negative impact on the morale of new hires.

She asked me, 'What do you think we should do about them?'

Immediately I replied, 'Tell them it's time to quit. And if they don't leave or shape up, fire them.'

She was shocked by my response. 'But they have a very strong union,' she said. 'And they have served so many years. Doesn't the airline owe them something for that?'

Again I shared my strong views:

'Find them a meaningful role on the ground that harnesses their skills and experience to real advantage. If that doesn't work, or they won't do the work required, then fire them.

'And if you can't fire them because of union, then create a "Department of Dead Wood" and park them inside until they retire. They'll still cost the airline in payroll accounts, but at least they won't cause so much damage.

'As for the airline "owing them something", hasn't the airline been paying the crew, training and rewarding them all these years? Haven't the airline and crew members grown up together?

'Everyone shares good feelings for achievements and successes in the past. But shouldn't we share responsibility, too, for building a strong and successful future?'

The supervisor was not comfortable with my answer, I could tell, but it certainly got her thinking.

What about you?

Key Learning Point

When someone on your team loses his or her enthusiasm or commitment, it's time for them to either change or go. This is especially true when that person is very senior and is looked up to as a role model by newcomers to the organization.

When you've lost the fire, it's time to retire.

Action Steps

Share this insight with everyone on your service team. Make it part of your staff orientation program so that new team members know what to expect of the elders.

Share this with your senior staff, as well. They must understand what it takes today to keep an organization going – and growing.

Serving others? Serve yourself!

Have you met service providers who are frustrated, tired or just burnt out?

They may look frantic or exhausted. They may sound sad or just plain bored.

Their pride in service has faded away and their passion has all but disappeared. They are just going through the motions, watching the clock, earning a living and waiting for the day's demise.

Have you met one of these tired men or women? Have you ever *been* one?

Serving others is the essence of a fulfilling business and social life. But service requires a contribution, an exchange of energy between two players.

You can't serve others well unless you've learned to serve yourself.

Key Learning Point

If you are too worn out to serve with a smile on your face and a glow of goodness in your heart, you need rest and rejuvenation right away. Do what's best for your customers – and for you. Take a break. Serve yourself.

Action Steps

Take a walk. Spend time with nature. Listen to music. Read and be inspired. Splurge on a favorite food. Get a backrub. Give a hug. Talk to an old friend. Drink something healthy. Take a short nap. Watch the clouds go by. Visit an art gallery or a playground. Take a class. Throw a party. Write a poem. Call your mother. Watch a movie that will make you laugh or cry. Step in the shower and sing out loud. Enjoy a long, hot soak in the tub.

Do whatever lifts you up, clears your mind and turns you back 'on' for delivering superior service.

Give the gift of giving

Our daughter, Brighten, is adored, admired, praised, encouraged, loved...and a bit spoiled.

Friends and family members bring her an unending stream of books, toys, stuffed animals and other gifts.

Here's the best practice I've seen for handling 'toy overload' in your child's playroom.

Tell your little one it's time to share 5 or 10 of her current toys with less fortunate children at a nearby orphanage, children's hospital or day-care center.

Let your child pick the toys to give away. Then bring your youngster along to make the actual donations. Let *your* child see the joy and gratitude in *another* child's face.

Start early and make it a family tradition.

Key Learning Point

Let your child experience the generosity and compassion that bring joy and well-being to others. Let her feel service as its own reward. Let her learn early how life gives back to those who give themselves.

Action Steps

Give your child the gift of giving. (And clean up the playroom, too.)

THE HEART OF THE MATTER

'Love is the essence of service and
our connection to one another.'

In the spirit of service

The 'Spirit of Service' Award is given to uniquely deserving teams and individuals who go way beyond the call of duty to serve, aid or comfort the heart of another human being.

One worthy winner is an unnamed night nurse in the maternity ward of a nearby hospital.

A new father wrote to me with this report:

'My experience at the hospital was very positive. I was staying over with my wife after the delivery. One night I had a headache (maybe from the lack of sleep and being a first-time parent). I asked one of the staff for a pain reliever. She gave me a neck rubdown for a few minutes instead! That really made me feel better, and no need for medication. I was impressed that the staff went out of her way to satisfy a "customer", even when I wasn't the baby or the mother. Is that good customer service or what?'

You bet it is! Three key characteristics of an 'UP Your Service Mindset' are: abundant generosity, genuine compassion and seeing the world from your customer's point of view. Whoever she is, this night nurse at the hospital clearly demonstrated all three.

Key Learning Point

To offer the spirit of service, look beyond your customer's request to identify their true concerns. What you can offer may be different, and more effective, than what they have requested. Listen for unspoken needs, not just spoken words.

Action Steps

Extend your care beyond the normal course of action. Serve your customers, and those they love, the way you would love to be served.

In customers we trust

I was in Boston and wanted to buy a homeopathic remedy for my young daughter. At 9:10 pm I drove up to a local health food store, Bread & Circus.

The store closed at 9:00 pm and cash registers were sealed for the night. But the manager could see my concerned face through the glass door and let me step inside.

He listened to my concern, then walked down the aisle, picked up and handed me the $10.95 product I needed and said, 'You can come back and pay for it tomorrow'.

I was amazed. He asked for my name and telephone number, but when I said I lived outside the United States, he replied, 'Well, just come back in the morning and tell them what you got. We open at 9:00 am.'

I was back in the store the next morning with a grateful smile, and $10.95, and a *big* compliment for Mike, the night manager of Bread & Circus.

Key Learning Point

Statistics (and common sense) show that most customers are honest, appreciative and sincere. Yet organizations are filled with strict policies to foil the few who might try to cheat.

Make your business a place of caring, connection and trust. Those you serve in an open manner will gladly return the gesture.

Action Steps

The next time *your* customer is in a tight spot, forgot his wallet, needs something extra now with only a promise for later, create a powerful and positive impression.

Take action on this oath: 'In customers we trust'.

Moment of truth or moment of impact?

Moments of truth are all those times when customers experience and evaluate your service. Work hard, do a good job, and customers will come back for more.

Moments of impact are those rare moments when someone goes way above the call of duty, stretches the envelope far beyond the stamp, innovates and takes action in unexpected ways that are valued, appreciated...and remembered.

A client at a seminar handed me this note: 'Last night, 10 minutes before departure at the airport, I found my car and house keys still with me, which means my wife would have been locked out of the house. I passed them to the Singapore Airlines in-flight supervisor and they managed to get the keys to her within the hour!'

This is a great moment of impact. If the airline was only in the business of flying passengers from city to city, they would miss the opportunity to *impact* this customer for life.

A client of Citibank was delayed for four hours overseas. He called the local Citiphone office at 2:00 am and asked them to call his wife six hours later...by which time she would be awake, but he would be 37,000 feet up in the air. The bankers made the call, and made the *impact*.

Key Learning Point

Moments of impact do more than just surprise your customers: they deepen the relationship, extend goodwill, increase tolerance of any future problems and build loyalty far into the future.

Action Steps

The next time your customer needs assistance that's outside your normal course of work, make the decision, make the effort – make the *impact*.

Helping others succeed is good service

I receive a lot of voice mail. Maybe you do, too.

Some folks leave nice and clear messages that are easy to understand. Others seem to be in quite a hurry, especially when they leave their phone number.

When returning calls, I make a point of praising those who leave clear messages. And I encourage the others to speak a bit more slowly, cautioning that 'hurried messages' are sometimes difficult to decipher. Rarely do 'fast speakers' know about the problem. After all, who leaves themselves a message on the voice mail?

Fax machines provide another opportunity to help each other. Have you ever received a fax with a dark vertical line running the length of the page? This is caused by specks of dirt stuck to the glass strip inside the *sender's* fax machine. But the person who sends the fax never knows about the problem. They never see the lines. After all, who ever sends themselves a fax?

Whenever a fax with 'long lines' shows up in our office, we make a point of contacting the sender, explaining how to open up the fax machine and quickly clean the glass.

It's not really our business, but then again, maybe it is.

Key Learning Point

All of us are partners with each other. If *you* help one person, maybe *I* will get the benefit down the line. If *I* help another, one day *you* may reap the same reward.

Action Steps

Look for ways you can help others to improve their service, accomplish their objectives, or simply do a better job.

Create your own 'Godiva moment'

One of the nice things about flying First or Business Class is the little 'extras' in the passenger experience: wider seats, soft slippers, interesting magazines, comfortable headphones, etc.

On a recent flight, a member of the cabin crew appeared after dinner with an elegant box of Godiva chocolates. She invited me to make a selection from the small but expensive temptations.

I replied spontaneously, 'Oh, thank you!'

Some of the chocolates were dark and round, others were light and square. One had a tasty looking nut on top. Two were wrapped in gold foil. I was flustered for choice. They all looked so good!

I asked the smiling crew member, 'Which is your favorite?'

She knelt down in the aisle next to my seat and looked over the selection. Pointing gently to a dark chocolate square with the Godiva logo on top she said, 'That one.' And then, 'But I like this one, too, and that one, also.'

I mentioned my preference for light chocolate over dark, which she followed with two more recommendations.

We looked at each other and laughed. We had chosen every piece in the box! It was a unique 'Godiva moment'.

'Let me get you a plate,' she said standing up, 'then you can try one of each.'

When she returned, we selected four Godiva chocolates for me to sample. The whole process was a treat. The sweets, and the service, were delicious.

Two weeks later I was flying on a completely different airline, also in an upper class of travel. After dinner a member of the cabin crew came by offering...Godiva chocolates!

The elegant box was exactly the same. But the service could not be more different.

As the crew member moved through the aisle, she made no eye contact whatsoever. There was no pleasure or invitation in her voice. She thrust the box first in one direction, then the other.

Her voice was barely a mumble: 'Chocolate? Chocolate? Chocolate?'

By the time she came to my seat, she had given up asking altogether and simply pushed the box towards my face. I saw the same range of chocolates as before, but had no appetite whatsoever for tasting.

My reply was as hollow as her invitation, 'No thanks'.

Key Learning Point

Anyone can provide a product. But only those with a passion to serve will offer an experience of pleasure. Quality service is about making the connection, not handing out the chocolate. It's about leveraging the contact, not just pouring the coffee. It's about being the person that people remember, not simply doing a procedure, pushing a policy or wrapping up a purchase.

Action Steps

Look carefully at your products. How can you make them more attractive? What can you do to enhance their appeal? Can you make them a bit more 'Godiva'?

Now study your presentation, people and procedures. Could they be smoother, more pleasant or friendlier? How can you polish your service, give your customers a special treat, and create your own unique 'Godiva moment'?

Find and do your own thing

In quality manufacturing, speed requires standardization. No wonder Six Sigma, Zero Defects and ISO Certification receive so much time and attention.

But in quality service, doing something unusual or eccentric can create a powerful impact. In service, it can be quite acceptable to find and do your own thing.

Here are just a few examples:

A waiter at the Sugar Beach Resort in Mauritius comes to work each day with a thermometer in his pocket. On the way to the restaurant he takes the temperature of the ocean water and the swimming pool. As he pours coffee and clears plates during breakfast, he joyfully tells guests exactly how warm and enjoyable their swimming will be that day.

A room service attendant at the same resort noticed a guest from Germany reading Goethe during her stay. He got coaching from a colleague and learned a poem in German by heart. A few days later as he served her dinner in her room, he recited the poem proudly for her enjoyment.

A sales clerk at Nordstrom in the United States sold my friend a new pair of shoes. Measuring his feet, the clerk discovered my friend's right foot was size 9.5 and the left foot was a smaller 9.0. The clerk gave my friend the shoes he needed to achieve a perfect fit: one 9.5 and the other 9.0. I have no idea what the clerk did with the remaining mismatched shoes, but my friend's loyalty to Nordstrom has been secured.

The customer of a furniture maker in Malaysia returned one large item and selected another. A partial refund was due, but the customer was to leave the country that very night. One staff member offered to process the refund paperwork on the same day. At 8:15 pm he arrived at the customer's house with the refund check in hand...and a small cake with

'Bon Voyage!' written across the top.

At the Raffles Hotel, one laundry worker writes small notes complimenting male guests on the fine fabric of their suits and female guests on the elegance of their evening gowns. These notes are pinned gently to the garments before they are hung back in guests' closets after drycleaning. What a memorable moment!

At the Four Seasons Hotel, order a juice or soft drink from the bar. You'll discover ice cubes made from the same drink. As the ice melts your drink gets colder, but not diluted. You get a stronger drink. Strong service, too.

Key Learning Point

What is 'your thing'? Is it the personal note you attach to outgoing documents? Is it the enthusiastic tone in your voice on the phone? Is it your pride in teaching customers or colleagues something new? Is it as simple as the colorful clothes you wear, the magazine and newspaper articles you share with others, or your passion for indoor plants that makes the whole office come alive?

Action Steps

Whatever it is that turns you on, find and do your own thing. Then take it one step further. Turn 'your thing' into something special – to the advantage and enjoyment of others.

Say the magic words

There are moments in life when someone says just a few magic words that become powerful beyond the speaker's imagination.

Perhaps this has happened to you. It has to me – twice.

The first magic moment occurred in 1972 when my high school science teacher, Stan Rhodes, challenged his students to see who could build the strongest bridge using just a limited amount of balsa wood and glue.

On the day of the contest, a serious problem emerged. I knew the span of the bridge could be at least 12 inches, but I got the width wrong. I understood the maximum width was 1 inch. In fact, it was 1.5 inches.

While my design was good, my bridge was 33% thinner than all the others. Even so, it came in second place.

I was crushed. With an additional half-inch of width, I surely would have won the contest.

As I was leaving, Mr. Rhodes pulled me aside and said, 'Actually, your bridge had the best design. Well done.'

I looked up at him, my mood completely changed.

'Really?' I asked in surprise. 'Do you think so?'

'Absolutely,' he grinned. 'You are a very good designer.'

'Thanks, Mr. Rhodes!' I walked away triumphantly.

Today, more than two decades later, I make my living as an innovative curriculum designer. I've built bootcamps, orientation programs, international tours, interactive workshops, management retreats, conference games, video and web-based learning systems and more. I am confident and passionate about the power of good design.

Stan Rhodes' magic comment made a difference.

The second magic moment came when I was new to the business world, a recent graduate of my youthful years as a world-trotting citizen diplomat and Frisbee instructor.

I attended my first National Speakers Association Annual Convention. Nervous and inexperienced, I was under-dressed for the event and had no idea how successful speakers built their impressive careers.

By chance I stood next to Thomas Winninger in the back of a large conference room. Thom and I are about the same height and for an instant we saw eye to eye. He introduced himself with enthusiasm – his trademark. I offered a more hesitant 'Hello.' We chatted for just a short while. I felt rather awkward.

A few moments later, Thom looked right at me and spoke with an intensity that went to my core: 'I can see you've got what it takes to succeed in this business. You'll do well.'

It was a busy conference and Thom was very well known. We soon parted company in different directions. His comment, however, stayed with me.

Today, more than twenty years later, I enjoy my career as a successful professional speaker. Thom was right, I did have what it takes. I wonder how he saw it? Maybe he figured that anyone who showed up at the Annual Convention had the interest and desire, if not yet the skills required.

Then again, perhaps Thom didn't see much potential at all, but spoke up to help me create it.

Thanks, Thom.

Key Learning Point

What you say to another person may impact the balance of their lives. Make the effort to boost their confidence, self-image and esteem.

Action Steps

Don't hold back. Move other people forward. Say the magic words.

Turning provocation into pleasure

I appreciate it when people disagree with me. It shows they are thinking hard and often opens the door to new insights and learning on both sides.

Sometimes, though, the other person puts a sting into his message – a touch of caustic comment to perturb, provoke and discomfort.

I used to hit back at such remarks, using my own wit in defense, with a touch of offense for good measure. I've since found a better approach. Maybe you can use it, too.

A customer of Indian descent wrote criticizing me for the pricing of my video learning systems, all of which end with the number '8': $388, $288, $98, etc.

'8' is considered a fortunate number in many parts of Asia. (In Cantonese dialect, '8' sounds like the word for 'wealth'.)

He complained that I was trying too hard to 'please the Chinese', then commented cuttingly that my success in Asia might be due primarily to the fact that I am Caucasian.

To be honest, my first instinct was to fight back. But then I paused long enough to remember my values and positive commitments. Ultimately, here's what I wrote:

1. I thanked him, sincerely, for his feedback. Good, bad or ugly, when someone takes the time to write, it is already an expression of commitment.

2. I discussed the '8' issue, acknowledging that '.99' and '.95' are all intended to offer pricing *below* a round number threshold. I agreed with him that numbers ending with '8' were recognized and appreciated by the ethnic Chinese in my Asian customer base.

3. I then acknowledged how important *his* ethnic group is within the Asian market. I mentioned how enthusiastically and constructively Indians tend to participate in my interactive educational events.

4. I discussed the 'white man in Asia' situation and agreed that being an international talent allowed me an initial opportunity to present my skills. But this is not enough in the long term.

   The Asian business community is pragmatic and tightly networked. If *any* newcomer adds positive value and delivers more than expected, they will be frequently engaged and positively referred. If not, however, a negative reputation grows just as quickly, no matter what your pricing or the color of your skin.

   What matters in Asia, in business and in life, is what you have to offer, what promises and commitments you can make, and what you can deliver.

5. I added a small note about how many hours I work each week (plenty), and that the time spent replying to him I considered time well spent. He had communicated honestly with me, giving me a chance to communicate honestly in return.

A few days later, the same customer wrote back. He was surprised by my reply and was positive in his remarks.

Key Learning Point

The next time someone attacks you with a complaint, an insult or a comment loaded with 'bite', take a deep breath before you respond. Remember – and apply – the power of constructive communication.

Action Steps

Thank upset complainers for their feedback. Acknowledge what's *correct* about their observations. Point out what's *positive* about their point of view. Then provide your own key points, insights or explanation. You'll feel a lot better about the dialog. They will, too.

You may never know what's really going on

 We meet people face-to-face, at counters, in meetings, in writing and over the phone. Often our moments of contact are brief, fragmented, and mere snapshots in the longer movie of their lives.

We form impressions based upon these moments, and act upon those feelings. But we may never know what's really going on.

The next time you encounter someone who triggers a negative reaction by their tone of voice, body posture, odd request or persistent misunderstanding, take a moment to pause and consider.

This other person may have health or financial difficulties you will never know about. This other person may be in the middle of a crisis or some unanticipated trouble. This other person has a life that is not revealed by your short moment together. This other person may be a lot like you.

Given that I may never know 'what's really going on' with those who trigger my negative emotions, I've adopted two principles that serve me (and them) very well:

1. *Practice generosity*

   For the upset customer, I give something more than they expected. For frustrated staff, I offer an extra pat on the back. For the disgruntled vendor or supplier, I give them the benefit of the doubt.

2. *Exercise compassion*

   To the angry customer I say gently, 'You must be having a tough day.' To the befuddled sales clerk I offer, 'Thanks for your help. I know this can be confusing.' To the forever unsatisfied I state, 'It's OK. You deserve to get what you really want.'

Note that my principles are to *practice* generosity and *exercise* compassion. This isn't always easy. It takes effort, a bit like doing sit-ups. But it does get easier over time, and makes me feel better, too.

Key Learning Point

You win loyalty when people see you are on their side, not against them. The next time you experience a negative reaction to another person's words, actions or behavior, do some mental sit-ups before you reply. Then practice generosity and exercise compassion.

Action Steps

Discuss this with your colleagues, friends and family members. Find out what kind of person bothers, irritates or gets you hopping mad. Then brainstorm what might be happening or hurting in someone else's life that has them acting up or behaving towards you that way.

If you were in that painful position, what generous gesture or compassionate kindness might you appreciate most? What nice things could someone say that would help you out? What kind actions could someone do that would ease or heal your pain?

The next time someone upset or angry appears in your life, take the initiative to do something right: practice generosity, exercise compassion.

What to do when your customer is about to explode

When things go wrong, many customers get upset. Some blow up in anger. The next time your customer is ready to *explode*, use these five proven steps to sanity.

Step One: Let them blow off steam! No one is rational when they have pent up anger and emotion. Let your customer vent the rage and fury. Don't take it personally, and don't get in the way. Open a channel for them to let off the pressure.

Years ago I had a problem with a shipment by an express courier company. I called the company and got a reasonable sounding woman on the phone.

'You folks messed up!' I yelled.

'OK,' she replied in a very attentive tone.

'This was a really important shipment!' I continued loudly.

'OK,' she replied with concern.

'And my customer is going to be very upset,' I complained.

'OK,' she replied again a calm voice.

'Well, what are you going to do about it?' I finally asked, exhausted by my own tirade.

She paused a moment. 'OK?' she asked gently.

'OK,' I replied, smiling at her quiet but effective approach. And then we began the process of working things out.

Imagine if she had asked me for all the information right away! In my anger, it would have taken twice as long to give her the details, and extended my frustration, too.

Instead, she gave me the space and time to simply 'blow off steam', not taking it personally, allowing her angry customer (me!) to settle down.

Step Two: Show the customer you are 'on their side'. Let the customer know you are there to help, not to argue, defend or disagree. Phrases like these will work: 'Oh! I am really sorry to hear that. Can you tell me exactly what happened?' or 'I can certainly understand your frustration. Let me be the one to help you.'

Phrases to avoid are these: 'That's strange. It's never happened like that before. Are you sure that's what happened?' and 'It's not our policy to do anything over the phone. You have to write, fax or come in personally.'

Some words can trigger angry conversations. Avoid phrases like: 'Whose fault is this?' and 'Who is to blame?' or 'About your accusation...' These sound like a police investigation or a court case...which is *not* where you want to end up!

Step Three: Tell your customer exactly what you will do on their behalf. Explain what steps you will take, and when you will get back in touch with the results.

Step Four: Take fast action! Get the problem fixed. Resolve the misunderstanding. Champion the cause of your customer within your organization.

And when you do fix the problem, go the extra mile. Give them a bit more than they expect. They will remember and appreciate your efforts.

Step Five: Finally, go back to the customer and explain how the problem has been resolved. Ensure they are fully satisfied, and thank them for allowing you to help.

Key Learning Point

Angry customers can be effectively defused, and then well-served, with this proven, step-by-step plan of action.

Action Steps

Be sure all your staff understand and can implement these steps, especially under pressure!

As much as possible, forgive them

A busy restaurant manager attended my seminar on creating 'customer delight'. Soon after, she wrote to me directly, asking this most appropriate question:

Hello Ron,

I received a complaint from a customer about certain issues in our restaurant. After checking with the parties concerned, there was a lot of variance between what happened and the customer's version. We know the customer lied as we have documents to verify the facts.

How should I reply, as I am being chased by her for an official explanation.

Thanks & regards,

Serene

Here is my reply:

Hi Serene,

This happens all the time. The customer may be wrong, but let's keep in mind that she is still your customer.

You don't need to challenge her veracity or integrity (that would create a lose–lose situation). Instead, agree with her on the importance of the key value dimension in her complaint (speed, courtesy, flexibility, personal service, value for money, etc).

Then move on to your proposal to resolve or repair this situation. Show appreciation for her patronage and, frankly, ignore her lies.

If there is a financial dimension to this complaint and she wants a refund or compensation, provide some small token, voucher, future discount or special offer 'as a gesture of goodwill'.

I am assuming if you handle this right, she will come back in the future, speak positively about you and spend more money with you, too. These should be your ultimate objectives.

Sometimes customers can be jerks. As much as possible, forgive them.

All the best,

Ron

PS: If this approach does not work, let your customer know (as diplomatically as possible) that there must be some misunderstanding. Apologize for any confusion and then explain your view of the situation showing the records in your possession. (Do this gently. There *may* be a misunderstanding after all.)

PPS: If this still does not work, and your customer threatens inappropriate action, let her know (as diplomatically as possible) that you need to refer this to someone else for proper handling. Then pass it to your lawyers.

Key Learning Point

Sometimes customers will overstate a situation to the point where they lie. Restrain any urge you may have to attack or expose their exaggeration. Use kindness to counteract their offense, and generosity to overwhelm their guilt. Remember, no one wins an argument with a customer. If you lose the argument, you lose. And if you win the argument, you still lose.

Action Steps

Call a staff meeting to discuss ways your customers inflate, overstate or exaggerate. Acknowledge how your staff might feel when facing these situations. Separate the urge to 'fight back' from the stronger desire to create a positive outcome. Role play responses to achieve positive business results.

The customer is *not* always right. But the customer is always important. When your customers lie, opt for a higher plane. As much as possible, forgive them.

Handling customer abuse

Have you ever seen a customer who curses and screams, threatens, bangs the counter and throws things about? I have, and it's not a pretty sight.

An upset customer is understandable. An abusive customer is unacceptable.

If you encounter an irate customer who threatens, insults or barks foul language, use this approach to calm them.

Start by accentuating your intention to assist: 'Sir, I am here to *help* you. But it's hard for me to *help you* if you keep speaking to me that way.'

Try this several times. If they continue berating or attacking you personally, simply say: 'I would really like to *help* you, but I cannot do so when you speak to me this way. If you will calm down, *I can help you now*. Otherwise, please call me again later.'

If they calm down, help them. If they continue the abuse, hang up, or excuse yourself and walk away. If they become more furious still, call your supervisor (who should repeat the same steps), or security (who will take different steps altogether).

Key Learning Point

No service provider should endure ongoing customer abuse. We are in service to help, not get hurt. Defuse abuse with your clarity and commitment to serve. If that works, so can you. If it doesn't work, get yourself out of the way.

Action Steps

Train your staff thoroughly in how to defuse abusive customers, and when to call for help. Be sure everyone on your team is committed to preserving the dignity of everyone else, including the customer.

To inspire perfect service – tip!

Have you ever experienced lousy service? Ever had the pain compounded by staff who obviously expect a 'tip'?

I wonder what inspires people to provide customers with better service: anticipating a tip at the end of an interaction, or responding to a tip offered at the beginning?

I experimented to find out. Instead of evaluating service and then tipping when the service is very good (my usual practice), I tried tipping in advance, giving service staff a small gratuity at the *beginning* of each service interaction.

By tipping in advance I removed a question mark from the mind of the service provider ('Is this guy going to tip me?') and also from my own mind ('Should I tip this person? If so, how much?').

As I went proactively 'tipping through life', remarkable things happened. I noticed more smiles all around, plenty of extra-mile efforts on my behalf, and considerate personal follow-up throughout my travels.

Word spread quickly about me among staff in hotels and restaurants. People smiled more, or perhaps it just appeared that way.

Key Learning Point

When a service provider receives acknowledgment and encouragement from the very beginning, they may do much more to serve you well. Everyone appreciates being appreciated, occasionally in advance.

Action Steps

You, too, can enjoy better service. Express your appreciation early. Try tipping your way through life.

Nice work! Well done! Keep it up!

I like to (quickly) thank those who give me good service, and (gently) critique those who don't.

Here's an easy and effective way to do it.

I designed and then printed 250,000 laminated, full-color, wallet-sized cards that say: 'GOOD JOB! *Nice work! Well done! Keep it up!*' on one side, and 'CHEER UP! *A smile costs you nothing, but brightens up everything!*' on the other.

There's a big, bright yellow sun on the 'Good Job!' side, and a smaller timid sun peeking out from behind dark clouds on the 'Cheer Up!' side.

I took these cards on a recent trip and gave them to immigration officers, taxi drivers, airline cabin crew, room service staff and others. The impact was *amazing*! Eyes lit up and smiles appeared. Even those who did not speak English got the happy message right away.

Leaving one hotel, I asked the porter, 'Have I given you a "Good Job!" card?' He pulled out his wallet quickly. Opening it, he showed me a photograph of his wife and child, with a bright, sunny 'Good Job!' card right beside.

Key Learning Point

People everywhere appreciate recognition. Find a way to acknowledge those who serve you well, and raise the spirits of those who need your help. You don't have to provide therapy, give money or write long letters. A simple 'Good Job!' or 'Cheer Up!' card will do.

Action Steps

Visit www.RonKaufman.com/products.html to see the 'Good Job!' and 'Cheer Up!' cards. Order yours now – then pass them on!

3

THE SPIRIT OF THE TEAM

'To fly a flag of excellent service teamwork,
each person must stand tall and play their part.'

One shared voice to the customer

My friend Nancy was learning about her international callback service and exchanged e-mail with their office in Seattle.

She still had unanswered questions and e-mailed them once again.

The same person responded, suggesting that Nancy read the material they had sent. But Nancy had not received any materials, so there was nothing to read or study.

Once again, Nancy e-mailed her questions to Seattle. This time she got an abrupt reply: 'If you would read the material, you wouldn't have to keep bothering me.'

Nancy shot back, 'I never received the material. And whatever happened to customer service?'

The response from Seattle? 'I'm not in Customer Service. I'm in Sales.'

This episode illustrates one of the great challenges in business: how to get everyone thinking, speaking and acting as a coherent organization, presenting 'one shared voice' to the customer.

The challenge is inherent in the nature of specialized companies today. Precise engineers are hired for different tasks and purposes than the extroverts whooping it up in Sales. Detailed accountants are trained much differently than the expansive minds in Marketing and Communications. People in Production are measured differently from the team in After-Sales Service.

So what can *you* do to build an organizational culture where people understand one another and everyone works together? How can you build your team so the folks in Sales realize they are *also* in Customer Service?

Here's one set of proven and effective ideas. Try them!

- Use cross-functional teams to tackle persistent issues and organizational problems.
- Involve people throughout the company in joint training programs.
- Schedule time for frequent rotation and attachment of staff between various departments.
- Send cross-functional groups on 'mystery shopping' tours to competitive organizations.
- Get every department involved in focus group meetings to study customer compliments and complaints.
- Create a recognition program to praise cross-functional communication and improvements.
- Implement a reward scheme for everyone based upon overall company performance.
- Communicate customer issues to every person in every department through meetings, newsletters, e-mail, intranet and bulletin boards.

Key Learning Point

In the hustle of day-to-day business, many people focus largely on the job at hand. This narrow view may help them 'get their job done', but may also blind them to shared customer and company concerns.

Action Steps

Implement activities that encourage cross-functional sharing, caring and interdependence. Insist upon 'one shared voice' that understands and serves your customers.

'A' is for outstanding

One workshop participant asked this question:

'I'm designing a performance measurement system for our in-house technology team and have run into a disagreement with my boss.

'He would grade a support technician as 'A' if the Service Level Agreement (SLA) norms have been met, and 'A+' for any additional enthusiasm shown.

'I want to give only 50% for meeting the SLA norms since these are non-negotiable specifications. The remaining 50% I would give for enthusiasm, special assistance and ongoing development of the expert. What do *you* think?'

Here is my reply:

You need to clarify with your boss and the rest of the in-house team what an 'A' should actually stand for.

In most schools, 'C' is 'satisfactory' – which means all the 'non-negotiable' specifications have been met. I also refer to this as 'customer satisfaction'.

'B' is 'good' (B+ is very good) – which means all specifications are met and the work is done with some notable level of enthusiasm, individual initiative, etc. This is the domain of 'customer delight'.

'A' is for 'outstanding' – which is reserved for performance well above and beyond the call of duty. 'A' is for extra-mile effort that brings the customer, or the company, to a new level of performance.

'A+' is legendary, a breakthrough, a brand new benchmark for others to remember, admire and follow. This is where your customers become ambassadors, enthusiasts, fanatics and devotees.

To my mind, an 'A' should not be given for simply 'doing

the job'. 'Doing the job' is just expected, merely satisfactory. That's a 'C'.

Doing *more* than the minimum job is where higher grades should be awarded.

I recommend you bring together your in-house customers and the members of your technology support team. Encourage discussion. Let there be a healthy debate.

Ultimately, agree on what A, B, C, D and F will stand for in your unique context. Then grade accordingly.

Key Learning Point

Within an organization, departments may have very different opinions about how well they are doing, and how well, or poorly, other departments around them are performing. These disagreements stem from a lack of clear standards for evaluating internal service. This can lead to misunderstanding, inter-departmental tension and low motivation and morale.

Setting clear standards provides a platform for better communication. Raising standards over time is a pathway to continuous improvement.

Action Steps

If your department supports, relies upon or works closely with another department, call a meeting to review or create agreed service and performance standards.

Use these questions to get the conversation rolling: How do you know when you are doing a good job? How do you know when other departments are doing a good job? What do you consider 'satisfactory' inter-departmental performance? What constitutes 'above average'? What could another department do that would delight you, astound you or have you stand up and applaud?

This commitment to setting clear standards is useful for internal support situations. You can – and should – use this approach with your external customers, too.

Feedback is the breakfast of champions

Do you encourage customer feedback with hotlines, focus groups and in-depth customer surveys?

One car manufacturer was exposed for systematically hiding customer complaints over a period of thirty years. How would you feel buying an automobile from a company with a policy and culture like that?

With your suppliers, what kind of customer are you? If they make a mistake, do you tell them right away and give practical suggestions for improvement?

How frequently do you give feedback to your team members? Are they satisfied with once-a-year appraisals? Are you? Is that enough to keep your people motivated and improving?

Many organizations have shifted from basic 'boss-to-subordinate job reviews' to '360-degree evaluation'. These exercises include constructive input from superiors and subordinates as well as colleagues, customers and suppliers.

In '720-degree evaluation', each person being evaluated simultaneously appraises those evaluating him or her. These reciprocal exchanges allow a coordinated, quarterly flow of constructive compliments, critiques and suggestions.

Key Learning Point

A regular, vigorous dose of omnidirectional feedback helps individual employees – and teams – quickly learn, improve and grow.

Action Steps

What types of feedback do you give and receive? How frequently are you evaluated and coached on your performance? How often do you share your assessments with others? What steps can you take to improve the flow of constructive feedback to you, from you and all around you?

Four questions to boost collaboration

Building strong partnerships is big business. But it doesn't have to be a big problem.

You can initiate powerful improvements with your customers, suppliers, colleagues – even with your family members.

Just ask these four simple but powerful questions and listen *carefully* to the answers!

1. What would you like me/us to do *more* of?

2. What would you like me/us to do *less* of?

3. What would you like me/us to *start* doing?

4. What would you like me/us *to stop* doing?

The answers you receive reveal what other people value, and what bothers them, too. Armed with this precious information, take action to make things better.

Key Learning Point

Tighten bonds now with your customers, suppliers, managers, employees, colleagues, friends and family. These four simple questions will get a dialog going, and keep your relationships growing.

Action Steps

Call a meeting, send an e-mail, draft a survey or post a feedback form on your website. Ask for candid comments, study the replies, then launch into appropriate, appreciated action.

Co-pay is a win–win–win

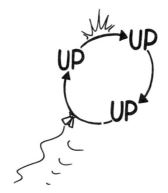

My first book, *UP Your Service!*, hit #1 on the national bestseller list within three weeks of release.

Thousands of copies have been purchased by individuals and companies around the world.

Where are all these books going!?

An increasing number are being purchased by organizations for each member of their staff. A bank in Dubai bought 650 copies. A government ministry in Hong Kong bought 500 copies for all frontline and back-office staff. The Young Entrepreneurs Organization ordered 450 copies for regional conference programs. An infrastructure consulting firm purchased 700 copies for every architect, draftsman, clerk and engineer. The Singapore Police Force purchased 1,200 books – one for every officer on the street.

Some organizations purchase the books outright and give them to the staff as a gift or take-home training aid. But others have adopted a unique approach of 'co-payment' – and the results have been astounding.

Instead of buying the books outright for their staff, these organizations pay only a *portion* of the price, with the balance to be paid by the staff themselves if they wish to own a copy.

The usual price is $25, discounted to $15 for orders over 100 copies. Most companies co-pay just $5, leaving the staff to pay twice that amount – $10 per book. To the staff it appears that $15 has been paid on their behalf.

What's the net result? Almost every staff member chooses to buy a book. Some get more than one copy for their spouse, friends and family members. Because staff members make a personal cash investment, they really do *own* and then study the book.

What's the payoff for the company? They pay only $5 per book, but their staff get a $25 training tool. It's a win–win–win situation. (The company wins, the staff win, and the author – that's me – also wins!)

The staff who buy the book tell me it's not just the bargain price that motivates their action. It's also the commitment their company shows by making the books affordable.

Companies tell me it's not just the special discount they appreciate, but the fact that staff members make a real commitment to read and learn and grow.

Key Learning Point

The co-pay option can be used with books, courses, meals, transportation, Internet access, home computers, medical care, accommodation, entertainment and more.

Action Steps

What does your organization care about? What do you want your people to believe and be committed to? Where can you use a co-pay option so that everyone shares an investment and an incentive to improve?

Get out of the Ivory Tower

Popeye's Chicken & Biscuits is a popular chain of more than 1,300 restaurants in 20 countries. They promote understanding between the people in head office and those in the restaurants with a range of vigorous and innovative programs.

In addition to a Customer Hotline and Mystery Shopper Program, they have a program called 'Getting In Touch'.

'Getting In Touch' helps staff from the Support Center (i.e. Corporate Headquarters) understand what day-to-day life is like in the restaurant. Support Center employees attend a two-day training session where they learn the basics of each restaurant station, including preparation, batter-frying, seasoning, counter and customer service.

They work at least one eight-hour shift in a restaurant each year, serving customers and spending time one-on-one with the Restaurant Manager.

Everyone at the Support Center gains hands-on appreciation for what happens in the restaurants every day. As a result, new programs, policies and procedures from the Support Center to restaurants in the field are appreciated, appropriate and effective.

Key Learning Point

To understand their staff and customers, those who work in head office must also spend time in the field.

Action Steps

Get your headquarters staff out of the Ivory Tower and into the trenches where real customer contact happens.

And think carefully about what you call the Corporate Office. Popeye's calls theirs the Support Center. What do you call yours?

Keeping in touch at Popeye's

Popeye's Chicken & Biscuits has launched another program called 'Keeping In Touch', in which Support Center employees contact Popeye's customers every month.

Their job is to follow up with customers who've complained *after* the Restaurant Manager or Area Manager has taken action to resolve the complaint.

This program enables those not working with customers on a daily basis to better understand vital customer issues. It also spurs managers at the restaurants to provide rapid service recovery.

These programs are simple yet powerful and positive. The restaurant managers feel well supported and understood. The people working in 'head office' feel responsible and in touch with the customer service process.

And happy customers get the best of both worlds: rapid attention, genuine concern and follow-through from all parts of the organization.

Key Learning Point

Getting in touch. Keeping in touch. Staying in touch. Good ideas. Good for business, too. After all, employees who understand are more productive. And customers who are well attended come back.

Action Steps

Design a similar program for your organization. Have your head office staff spend a day or two working in the field. Have your field staff spend a few days helping out at head office. Involve everyone in the customer contact and follow-through process.

Future sales are hiding in service

At the Repair and Service Center of a well-known technology company, customers are invited to examine and try the latest computers while waiting to collect their current systems.

Except for one problem: they don't *have* the latest computers on display!

Managers in the company's Sales Department have decided their latest products are better off on display only in the Sales Showroom in a completely different building across town. Why?

In the minds of the Sales Managers, the Repair and Service Center is merely a cost center for 'after-sales service', not a vital profit center for generating new business growth.

What an out-of-touch, narrow-minded, wasteful and expensive point of view!

Think about this: When you purchase a new policy or product, how much do you truly *trust* the salesperson offering the package?

Do you trust a salesperson from Company A any more than someone you meet from Company B, C or D? Not likely. After all, you know the sale is just the sale. Once your money has moved and the product is in your hands, any future problems will be addressed by the people in Service, not Sales.

On the other hand, if you do have a problem and someone from the Service Center responds quickly and generously to your needs, will you feel a higher level of trust and confidence in that person? for that department? It's likely that you will.

Customer Service staff *earn* your trust by appreciating your problems, showing empathy for your frustration, taking action on your behalf and staying in touch with you throughout the process.

If they follow up afterwards to ensure you are well and

truly contented, your level of confidence could go sky high.

Smart companies leverage that confidence into new leads, immediate referrals, high-value testimonials, positive word of mouth, increased sales...and growing profits.

Key Learning Point

Strong service systems and well-trained staff will earn your customers' trust. Seize the opportunity you deserve. Build upon that trust – and turn it into sales.

It doesn't matter what you sell: cars, computers, credit cards, insurance or home entertainment systems. Give your service team the tools and training and rewards they need to leverage hard-earned customer confidence into well-deserved and profitable new business.

Action Steps

Review your current structure for generating sales and providing customer service. If they are far apart or separated by opposing 'profit center' and 'cost center' mindsets, you are leaving precious revenue behind. Get the two connected!

After all, what's more important: protecting your existing structure, or creating more confidence and commerce with your customers?

Service begins in sales, new sales begin in service

How often is the Sales team on one side of an organization while Service is on the other?

How often does this 'divide' lead to the loss of possible sales, more tension between the groups, and negative service experiences and perceptions for the customer?

At one high-end European car dealer, the physical separation between Sales and Service was so thick, they called it the Berlin Wall.

It doesn't need to be this way!

In a bold effort to bring these groups together, the car dealer *tore down the physical wall* separating Service from Sales.

The sales staff were concerned. They were afraid new business prospects might be turned off by what they saw in the Service Department.

The service team was equally unsure, afraid of frequent and furious criticism from their colleagues in sales.

We need to change these points of view!

When you buy a new car, when do you want to meet the people in the Service Department? Do you want to wait until your first problem, tune-up or oil change? By that time you might be 'just another customer' needing service.

How would you feel if the people in Sales introduced you proactively and personally to the manager of the Service Department? Would you prefer the Service Manager know your name, greet you face-to-face and match you with your new car *before* you ever needed his assistance? I would.

A proper, positive, proactive introduction to the Service Department can have a huge impact on the experience and satisfaction of the customer. This makes sense: *good service begins in sales.*

Service is also a great time to begin new selling!

Experienced service professionals know a lot about the latest products and features. They know which models are popular, reliable and trouble-free, and they know which ones have problems.

If someone is repairing your machine and tells you about a newer model that is trouble-free and getting great reviews, would you be interested in learning more? Would you trust this person to be telling you the truth? Would you be willing to see or try a demonstration?

'Good morning, Mr. Kaufman. Your car is scheduled for a tune-up. We should have it ready by four o'clock. By the way, some new cars came in that handle just the way you like, and have the extra space you need for your sports equipment. I thought you might enjoy driving one. I reserved it for you to use while we repair the car you're driving now. Have a good afternoon. Enjoy your new car!'

It's true. *New sales can get started in service.*

Incidentally, the European car dealer is doing more than just tearing down the wall. They are changing the compensation program to pay salespeople when customers get great service, and pay service people when the Sales team sells more cars. It's a great way to get people's attention. And a smart way to get them working more closely together.

Key Learning Point

For more sales, better service, happier customers and employees, get Sales and Service working hand in hand. Customers experience both sides – each should support the other.

Action Steps

How well integrated are your Sales and Service teams? Do they work together to create positive service impressions and stimulate new sales? What can *you* do to tear down the wall between these two departments?

Winning and losing in the pit stop

Frontline service providers are key drivers in great service organizations. But don't forget the power of the 'back-end' to win or lose the race!

In every insurance company you'll find actuaries, policy administrators, IT professionals and clerical support staff. These folks have little contact with external customers, but they can certainly set the mood and the pace for the insurance agents and brokers who work out in front.

In a theater you enjoy actors on stage. But there would be no play without writers, directors, set design, lighting and make-up.

In a restaurant you meet the waiter and host or hostess, but without cooks, dishwashers and accountants, you'd never get a meal.

Car races are often won and lost by mere tenths of a second. The winners have great drivers, but also top performing pit crews who change oil, tires and fuel.

Southwest Airlines (famous in the United States for friendly front-line service) puts equal value on back-end support. Their benchmark for getting planes unloaded, reloaded and back in the air is the pit crew (not the driver) at the Indianapolis 500.

Key Learning Point

To win in the front you need great support in the back.

Action Steps

If you work on the frontline of service, give extra appreciation today to those who support you behind the scenes. If you work on the back-end, remember the power you have to boost the motivation and morale of those who work out front.

Literally 'burying the hatchet'

Relations between two departments had deteriorated badly over the years.

One was a state government agency, the other from the private sector. The culture of these two 'partners' could not have been more different.

At a team-building workshop, top managers from both sides decided to 'bury the hatchet'.

They bought a large, new hatchet at the hardware store in town. On one side, the government agency wrote their festering complaints. On the other, the private sector group wrote their protests, moans and grumbles.

After agreeing to work more positively in the future, both sides held a ceremony on the lawn. With photographers present, they dug a deep hole and literally 'buried the hatchet'. This symbolic ritual sent a strong, positive signal that the past was past. Both sides took responsibility for the future.

Can you *see* these two teams standing next to a pile of fresh dirt? Can you *hear* their pledge to start again anew? Can you *feel* the commitment as they walked away from a ceremonial hole in the ground?

Key Learning Point

To overcome old wounds you may need to work on a symbolic level.

Action Steps

Think about where your partnerships could be improved. Find a common phrase that captures the solution: 'bury the hatchet', 'patch things up', 'water under the bridge'. Perform a ceremonial rite or ritual that engages everyone in a gesture of new work and healing.

4

LISTEN TO THE LANGUAGE

'The words you choose to speak and hear will shape the
life you live. Choose wisely for a lifetime of service.'

Will this settle the case?

I wrestled with a computer manufacturer about a technical issue that required a simple solution. During the process I made suggestions on how the company could improve their procedures and service recovery efforts.

Time dragged on and messages accumulated back and forth. After several weeks, I was eager to get the whole thing over and done. Finally, the company's Customer Advocate made an appropriate offer of action and compensation and asked me, 'Will this settle the case?'

I listened to his language and sighed. This company just didn't get it.

Listen to the language: 'Will this settle the case?'

Does this sound like a customer-friendly organization taking care of an inconvenienced customer? Or is this a law firm, a police blotter, an insurance company settling a claim?

'Settle the case' means to put it down, stop the dialog, end further communication. It certainly doesn't sound like they want my future orders.

This company is not alone. I've been teaching another computer maker how to *increase* loyalty while responding to customer complaints. This company is committed to setting things right, and fast! They track exactly how long it takes to effectively 'close the case'.

But again, listen to the language: 'How quickly can we close this case?'

'Closing the case' means to shut the door, turn away and focus on something (or someone) else.

If you are a customer do you want your 'case closed'? Or do you want your problems resolved, your concerns addressed, your discomfort carefully attended?

'Will this close the case?' or 'Will this completely resolve your concerns?'

Which approach would bring you back? Which would boost your confidence, loyalty, repeat business and positive word of mouth? You choose.

Listen carefully to the language used inside *your* company. Do you hear commitment to a great customer experience, or compliance with company procedures?

'Handling customer complaints' or 'Responding to customer concerns'? You choose.

'Your application is being processed' or 'Your account will be opened soon'? You choose.

Which department do you want working on your behalf: 'Customer Affairs', 'Customer Service' or 'Customer Care'? You choose.

Key Learning Point

Language shapes and reveals the mindset of your team. If your customers are 'handled', 'processed', 'settled' and 'closed', you may not hear from them again. But if your customers (and staff) receive 'care', 'response', 'service' and 'support', they are likely to return with enthusiasm, testimonials and new business.

Action Steps

Conduct an audit of your company's terms, titles, jargon and language. Find every instance where customers have been degraded to 'cases' and concerns have been reduced to 'complaints'. Invent another way to speak about the people you serve, the promises you make and the experiences you create.

Make your language sound sweet, sensitive and sincere. When taking care of human beings, it does make a difference.

Well then, who do you do it for?

I enjoy high-end music systems in my home and office.

One day I called the dealer to order extra CD cartridges, wanting to pre-load them with different music. He was out of stock, but said more were coming soon.

'Great!', I replied, 'Could you give me a call as soon as they come in?'

He was reluctant. 'They'll be coming in a few weeks. Why don't you call us back then?'

With my travel schedule, I imagined missing the next shipment and asked again if he would call me. I reminded him that we had purchased $7,000 of equipment from his shop.

When I mentioned our address, he replied, 'I remember you. Well, as a personal favor, I'll try to give you a call, but we don't usually do this for customers.'

I was stunned. If not for customers, who do they do it for?

Key Learning Point

Quick outbursts from employees often reveal the real mindset lurking behind a surface smile. Have you ever heard someone say:

'We can't do that for you. It's not our policy. I'd like to help you, but it's not my department. You have to speak to someone else.'

Remember, serving customers is why you go to work. If your customers disappear, your positive future may vanish, too.

Action Steps

Listen for phrases that reveal a mindset of 'I just can't be bothered.' Identify them, then eliminate them.

When you shop, keep your ears well tuned. If they don't truly want to *serve you well*, take your precious business somewhere else.

Is the customer really king?

We often hear 'the customer is king'. I don't believe it.

First, many customers do not behave like kings. Some act more like ruffians than royalty. You might want to disregard this kind of customer altogether. But it's tough to disregard a king.

Second, in certain cultures, the king was revered but also feared. Hardly the best metaphor to bring closeness between your customers and your staff.

Third, the idea of a king implies that everyone else is not. I don't see the benefit of putting your customers on a throne if it means you and your team must live below them.

Perhaps it makes more sense to say 'the service provider is king'. I mean this in the most responsible way.

A benevolent king once traveled his realm in the disguise of a common man. He went to see for himself the quality of life his people experienced each day. Upon his return he made the changes required. If the streets were dirty, he had them cleaned. If a government office was ineffective, he had it fixed. If the people lacked some important goods or service, he arranged for needed improvements.

Key Learning Point

If you were the benevolent king or queen, reigning over your service domain, what changes would you make for the better?

Royal Action Steps

Search your organization in the disguise of a common customer. Visit your company website. If it's slow or confusing, get it fixed. Call your service department. If the help is not personal and pleasant, make it so. Access your information hotline. If you find a telephone tree more frustrating than functional, take out your royal shears and prune it.

It's a lose–lose–lose situation

One customer complained when served by a 'Trainee' at a five-star hotel. If served by someone not entirely qualified, he wondered, should he pay a less-than-qualified rate?

I think 'Trainee' badges are horrendous. They are frequently old and mangled, handed down from new staff to new staff for years.

The new staff feel exposed and humiliated, as if they do not warrant a real name until they prove their mettle on the front line. The customer feels uncertain and wary, wondering if his requests for service will be understood and acted upon correctly. And the manager is anxious, hoping a recycled plastic badge will provide some defense or insurance from customer upsets and complaints.

Just the opposite often happens. The staff, manager and customer are all on edge. It's a 'lose–lose–lose' situation.

Instead, train your new staff to welcome customers with solid eye contact and a warm smile while saying:

'Hello! It's good to have you with us today, and my pleasure to serve you. I'm still a bit new here so my colleague will be overseeing my work to be sure we take care of everything just the way you want it. Is that alright?'

Most customers would be surprised by such confidence from a new staff and are likely to respond, 'That's fine!' And if the service is good, positive compliments will surely follow.

Key Learning Point

'Trainee' badges don't help; they only hurt and hinder.

Action Steps

Don't create anxiety with an old piece of plastic. Instead, build confidence and goodwill with the right kind of training.

Keeping high tech, high touch

Years ago, the popular website at www.RonKaufman.com was up-graded to more powerful servers.

The site includes a library of articles about service quality, partnerships and customer-focused culture. You can view these online, or have them sent to you by e-mail autoresponder.

On the old server, requested articles were sent via e-mail from *robot@RonKaufman.com*.

On the new server, requested articles were sent from *librarian@RonKaufman.com*.

This is a tiny difference (*robot* vs. *librarian*), but it speaks to a larger issue. You *touch* my website when you visit and make a request. I don't want a *robot* touching you back.

The tug between high tech and high touch is longstanding. In the early days, mainframes exchanged data with 'dumb terminals' – okay language for computer techies, but not very friendly for the masses.

When distributed computing expanded to every desktop, it might have been called 'core–satellite computing' or 'cen-tral–local computing'. But someone paid attention, and 'client–server computing' was born. People language. Hu-man language. Comfortable language.

Key Learning Point

My friend Cathy sent me a note: 'Even though we weren't friendly before, her page on the high school website made me laugh. We've been in e-touch ever since.' Nice touch – *e-touch* – making technology more human.

Action Steps

When you change customer processes to include more technology and automation, remember that *real people* use your innovations. It's already a high tech world. Keep the language *high touch*.

Unsuccessful applicants deserve good service too

When you hire new staff, or put projects out to bid, do your advertisements state: 'We regret only selected applicants will be informed.'?

Think about this policy from the applicant's point of view. What a horrible fate to endure. As days go by, hope slowly withers and turns to anxiety, resignation or despair.

Would it be so difficult for your company to call, send a letter or a simple e-mail thanking unsuccessful applicants for their time – and wishing them all the best?

Unsuccessful applicants are active members in the ever-changing business world. They might apply for another position with you in the future. Perhaps they will talk about their experience of your company among their friends and family members. Perhaps they will form an impression of what your company is really like based upon how long they waited for a reply...but never heard a word.

Key Learning Point

Quality service should extend to everyone, even those you choose *not* to engage or hire. Applicants demonstrate an active interest in your organization. Let them know you appreciate their effort.

Action Steps

Examine the full range of your company communications. Look for situations where people are left unknowing and out-of-touch; missing callbacks, late updates, absent acknowledgements and more. Find the gaps and close the loops. Your reputation will grow and your culture of quality service will improve.

The power of a pregnant pause

The busiest maternity hospital in the world is my client. They were once listed in the *Guinness Book of Records* for 'most babies delivered in one year'!

Pregnant women appreciate the slow pace of elevator doors at the hospital, but visitors and guests complain, 'The elevators close too slowly!'

The slow doors are intentionally programmed to give pregnant women and wheelchair-bound patients more time to enter and exit. If the hospital were to speed up the program, you can imagine the complaints: 'The elevator doors close too fast!'

What would you do in this situation? Go faster? Stay slow? Endure the ongoing complaints? This hospital tried a more creative and cooperative approach.

Attractive signs were posted in the lobby and inside each elevator car saying: 'Thank you for assisting patients who may require extra time to reach the elevator. Your kindness is appreciated.'

Suddenly, slow elevator doors become a gesture of care and concern for others, while visitors 'in a hurry' are just as quickly included in a gracious social effort.

Key Learning Point

Sometimes the facts of the matter don't need changing at all – only the way we look at them needs to shift.

Action Steps

If something is bothering you or your staff, your visitors, guests or customers, see if you can shift the language and change the point of view. It's one powerful, effective way to change a situation.

Who loves the taxman?

The old saying goes, 'No one loves the taxman', but if I must pay taxes, the people at the Inland Revenue Authority of Singapore (IRAS) are the folks I'd rather pay them to.

IRAS boasts one of the best programs I have seen for building an energized and dedicated service culture.

They have a challenging vision ('To be the leading tax administration in the world'), clear and appropriate core values and a deep commitment to training. They recognize staff who perform well and have an active staff suggestion scheme.

Other workplace innovations include top-of-the-line computer equipment in highly personalized work spaces (I've never seen so many Winnie-the-Poohs in one cubicle in my life!), in-house sports and lounge facilities, a childcare center, an upbeat IRAS choir (!), regular inter-department games in the main lobby after office hours, free fruit once a month for all staff, a subsidized cafeteria, and more.

All this culture-building effort really works. Staff commitment to quality service and continuous improvement runs high. One staff member even suggested putting, 'It was a pleasure serving you' on the back of their business cards.

While the corporate culture is service focused, the language of tax administration seems to change more slowly.

IRAS still talks about 'taxpayers' who must 'comply' with their 'obligations' or else be in 'violation' and get charged a 'penalty'. That's hardly a friendly way to talk with someone you are committed to serve.

Why not change this language altogether? The IRAS could 'help companies and individuals fulfil their financial responsibilities to the nation in a complete, accurate and timely manner'.

Let's face it, most people would prefer to pay no tax. But if you are successful in business, investments or earning personal income, your success is partly due to the location where you make your money. The government structure and physical infrastructure are built and maintained by your taxes. It's that simple. It's an exchange, a collaboration, a partnership.

The term 'taxpayers' sounds like something out of the Middle Ages, when the King would send his hated 'Tax Collector' on a big, dark horse into town.

People at restaurants are not 'food eaters', they are appreciated diners.

People at hotels are not 'bed sleepers', they are welcomed guests.

People needing doctors are not 'medicine takers', they are valued patients.

People helping others are not 'time givers', they are respected volunteers.

And people who fulfill their financial responsibility where they live, work and earn income should not be labeled 'taxpayers', they are contributors, collaborators, partners. They are allies in the future of the nation. Shouldn't we refer to them this way?

Key Learning Point

Successful culture building should extend deeply into the language you use about yourselves and those you serve. Language shapes reality and the mindset of your staff.

Action Steps

If you are one who believes that 'No one loves the taxman', turn your own language and thinking around.

So you've got to pay taxes? What a happy problem. It beats being broke with no income and nothing to pay.

An apple a day keeps the customer

A large grocery store opened a new outlet in my neighborhood. A small basket of red apples sits by the cash register. The sign in the basket reads:

'Free apple if our staff at check-out did not greet you and say thank you.'

But the apple basket stays *full*. Not because the check-out staff are always smiling (trust me), but because the act of taking an apple is tantamount to 'catching the staff doing something wrong'! Who wants to irritate grocery check-out staff when they're ringing up your order?

To get the impact the store *really* wants, the sign could be re-written like this:

'Thank you for shopping with us. We want you to have a good shopping experience. If, at any point, we are so busy serving you that we forget to greet you or say "Thank you!", please let one of these delicious apples put a smile upon your face. We will smile back!'

The store would give away more apples with this sign, but would gain more smiles, too. Better text, better impact.

Key Learning Point

Follow your good ideas all the way from concept to detailed execution. Good ideas need great implementation to deliver real results.

Action Steps

Find where your promotions and policies are actually seen and heard by your customers. Be sure the message is as clear at point of contact as it was when first created.

Pick the words with power

Who wrote your company's vision, mission and value statements? Was it some long-forgotten committee, or a retired management team, or an advertising agency no longer on the job?

In too many organizations, these essential statements are leftovers – flat, dull and boring. Let's face it, no one is inspired by a predictable list of core values like teamwork, integrity and customer focus.

Instead, have your team choose powerful words and phrases that truly turn them on. Here are two examples:

Media Arts rides a digital wave in creativity and business focus. Here are three of the core values they have chosen:

'It's not work.' (They have much too much fun for that!)

'Sure we can do it! What was the question?' (These folks are committed, passionate and always eager to learn.)

'We grow with you.' (They turn customers into partners.)

Singapore Network Services dropped two thousand words of bland corporate text and created ten new statements to guide their group behavior. Here are three that stand out:

'Beep-Beep!' (Think Road Runner. These guys are fast!)

'Beyond the call of duty.' (They stretch, stay late, hustle.)

'Every customer is our customer.' (No departmental silos. Every customer gets full benefit of the entire organization.)

Key Learning Point

Keep your guiding statements fresh, relevant and inspiring.

Action Steps

Are your guiding statements up to date? Do they really turn your people on? If so, you grow. If not, you'll rot. Pick up the pen and start again.

Standing out in the crowd

The colonial post office in Singapore's financial district has been transformed into the luxurious Fullerton Hotel.

I worked with the first management team to craft vision, mission and value statements that stand out in a crowded hospitality market.

The vision is bold and clear: 'To be the best independent hotel in the world.'

The mission is brief yet potent: 'The Fullerton Hotel is an inspiration in the heart of Singapore.'

The core values are a trio of direction and motivation:

Loyalty: to guests, to the hotel, to each other, to the hotel industry, to Singapore.

Energy: being proactive, taking the initiative, showing enthusiasm, living and working with zest.

Growth: career growth, personal growth, growth of top-line revenue and bottom-line profits, growth of the hotel's reputation.

Key Learning Point

A few words can make a big difference. If you worked in the hospitality industry, would you be keen to learn more about this unique hotel? Of course! If you travel to Singapore, would you like to spend a few nights in their care? Absolutely. If you live in Singapore, would you host a dinner or plan a meeting at a location that promises to be 'an inspiration'? You bet.

Action Steps

Make sure the vision, mission, core values and guiding principles of your organization are at least this clear, motivating and effective. Make it so and you will grow.

A promise to remember

Kodak Polychrome Graphics (KPG) is a leader in the field of hardcopy reproductions: black & white, color, gloss, matte, large format, high-resolution, digital input, high-speed output, waterproof, sunproof and printing on demand.

Their customer requirements are constantly changing. (I'll bet yours are, too.)

In such a fluid business environment, KPG makes a promise to customers that is clear, confident and focused.

Our Promise

To be a company that changes technology. Not just a company that changes with it.

To be where our customers are. Here and around the world.

To be a company that focuses on one industry. Our customers' industry.

To anticipate our customers' needs. And exceed them.

To be a partner. Not just a vendor.

Last, but far from least, to be a company that keeps its promises.

I like this statement for two reasons: it is well articulated, and acknowledges the need for ongoing change.

Key Learning Point

The world is evolving daily. Your promises must progress, too.

Action Steps

Write a promise for customers that prepares them, and you, for an unfolding and challenging future.

Satisfaction-plus for a better world

Advanex (formerly Kato Spring) is a global company with head offices in Japan. They make every kind of spring you can imagine, from microscopic chip connectors to monster steel coils for securing aircraft cargo doors.

Paul Kato, grandson of the founder, insists upon vigorous 'glocalization' – adapting global concepts in local language to impact, educate, motivate and align scores of Advanex teams around the world.

At their annual Global Leadership Forum, I helped draft key statements for each group. Here are some examples:

The Group Mission is open-ended: 'Satisfaction-plus network for a better world.' Everyone understands they are part of a larger whole.

The Corporate Office Mission is also unique: 'To provide "Eureka!"' How many corporate offices promise and deliver such excitement?

For the Corporate Communications Department: 'Free Flowing.' (Their job is to move ideas throughout the network. No congestion here.)

For the factories and offices around the world, the language was selected to arouse local interests and concerns.

A few examples:

For Singapore: 'It's Value Time!' (Singaporeans are passionate about gaining value, and saving time.)

For Malaysia: 'World Class Team, World Class Results.' (Malaysians are always inspired by achieving 'World Class' status.)

For Hong Kong: 'Making tomorrow happen today.' (Hong Kong is a key to China's future, but is committed to real profits right now.)

For England: 'Shaping the future with pride.' (From the country that created Rolls Royce, what other articulation could suffice?)

For California: 'Create opportunities, increase satisfaction.' (Created for a team of recent immigrants to the United States.)

For Japan: '365-24-7-1.' (The company promises instant availability and immediate response. Get the message?)

Key Learning Point

Every group and culture is turned on by unique goals and aspirations. This is true of national and ethnic groups as well as specific occupations. The mission of your team should articulate the aspirations and desires of your players.

Action Steps

Review the statements of intention and direction for your company, department and position. Make sure they acknowledge the aspirations and harness the desires of those involved.

Australian service gets hopping

Australia welcomed the world for an Olympic extravaganza in 2000. This international event galvanized the nation to provide extraordinary service.

When the Olympics ended, the world went back home. Australians continued serving one another.

I toured the nation on a book promotion tour and discovered that 'complaining about lousy service' had become a national pastime. Every media interviewer focused on 'service horror stories'. Every call-in radio listener had an axe to grind, a tale of woe, a complaint to groan about.

The national language is peppered with phrases that acknowledge this unique situation:

'The Tall Poppy Syndrome' refers to how those who stand out by trying harder, get cut down by others instead.

'Bundee On/Bundee Off' means working when you're on the clock, but not a moment after.

'A fair day's work for a fair day's wage' says you only work as hard as you're paid for, but not a dollar more.

'She'll be right' means take it easy, don't hustle too hard, everything will work out over time.

One workshop participant raised eyebrows and concern when he said, 'Australia needs a recession. Only then will we understand the importance of giving our customers excellent service.'

He may have a point.

Customer service in Hong Kong was notoriously unfriendly ...until the 1997 financial crisis dropped retail spending to the floor.

Overnight, shop assistants and restaurant waiters learned how to smile and say a sincere 'Thank you!' to their customers. Hong Kong people learn and adapt very quickly.

The Asian economy bounced back a few years later, and that was good news for Hong Kong. The improved level of customer service continued. Good news for customers, too!

I don't think Australia needs (or wants) an economic recession, but the country could benefit from a clear statement of service intention and direction. Here's one suggestion:

Australian service – with a smile.
We're ready to go the extra mile!

Key Learning Point

Common language is often encumbered with negative words and phrases. Many are historical and deeply embedded in the culture. Don't let them dictate the quality of your future. Individuals, departments, companies – even countries – need an uplifiting way of speaking about ever-improving service.

Action Steps

Review the sayings and slogans you use each day. Keep those that align you towards the goal. Change those that take you off the track.

You get a little more when you come to Singapore

Singapore aspires to be a nation that provides consistently superior service. But the local population faces two fundamental problems.

First, a fear of losing runs deep within the culture. The local phrase *kiasu* highlights an urge to acquire more and a hesitation to give anything away.

Second, the population has been well trained to follow instructions with precision, but is less certain about taking new risks or innovative actions.

An expression is needed to challenge the nation, set the tone and give a new direction; a rallying cry to aim the country towards generosity and frequent innovation.

I have a proposal that just might work, an articulation with national purpose.

You get a little more when you come to Singapore.

This phrase raises the standards and points the way towards continuous and generous improvement.

Key Learning Point

No challenge is too large to improve, fine-tune or resolve. We can work on the environment, international cooperation, worldwide nutrition, free education, comprehensive medical care, cultural harmony and respect. But we need to know where we're trying to go. Clear articulation is a guidelight for the future.

Action Steps

What aspect of your work or life would you like to change most? Have a clear vision of what you want to achieve. See the challenges that lie before you. Now create the words that show you the way, and take actions to keep moving forward.

5

GENERATING NEW IDEAS

'Sustaining great service requires a continuous
flow of upbeat, innovative ideas.'

Is consensus sinking your organization?

The senior manager of a large organization called me seeking help.

'We are stiff and bureaucratic,' he said, 'but we want to be more open. We are formal until it hurts but we'd like more innovation. Can you help us, Mr. Kaufman? Can you share a new perspective and bring some fresh ideas?'

I accepted the assignment and found that what he said was true: they had an old culture of top-down control, suffocating authority, miles of red tape and rigid ways of working.

With enthusiasm, I prepared a speech that opened many eyes. Laughter rolled through the audience, self-reflection mixed with humor. I saw skepticism and resignation, but also interest, possibility and a desire for new action.

The next day my telephone rang. Someone in the audience felt I had gone too far, was too provocative, had challenged too many sacrosanct assumptions.

I was concerned, of course, but also began to wonder. Had I stayed within the safety zone of caution and consensus, would my remarks have hit the spot at all; would my speech have made a difference?

My friend Chauncey Bell opened *my* eyes on this topic with a point of view I found completely unexpected. He said, 'There are two times when consensus is required. First, when there is fundamental distrust in the group. Second, when you want to guarantee a lack of innovation.'

That statement caught *my* attention! I can understand why consensus works when distrust prevails within a group. After all, if everyone agrees on everything, then anyone will notice anything out of kilter.

It was the second half of Chauncey's claim that made me think much harder. If we cherish consensus and complete agreement, where is the space for 'out of the box' new thinking and 'off the wall' ideas?

It is risky to try something new, change from one day to the next, do something now you have never done before. But the world is changing day by day and innovation is all around us.

The most risky approach to your group's success may be trying to achieve consensus!

Key Learning Point

To say you seek innovation – but also want consensus – can be a recipe for frustration and confusion.

'Don't rock the boat' used to be the safest path to find the future and climb the company ladder. Today, a boat that won't rock is very likely sinking!

Action Steps

How open are you and your organization to completely new ideas? How welcoming are you to diversity, controversy and well-intended provocation?

If there are questions you cannot raise, issues you dare not discuss or items banned from your agenda, make the space and time to relook and reconsider.

The playful policy review

This bizarre report arrived from a perturbed customer in Asia:

'I wanted to play golf at a prestigious course in town, so I went to the Pro-Shop to book a time.

'The attendant at the counter said she could not take my booking in person as she was only allowed to accept golf reservations by telephone.

'I explained that I wanted to make a booking right away. And since I was already there, wouldn't she please make the reservation?

'The attendant refused once again, repeating that she only took bookings by telephone.

'A public telephone stood in the corner nearby. I walked over to it and promptly called the Pro-Shop. The attendant answered the telephone and proceeded to make my booking. The entire time I could see her at the counter while we were speaking on the phone. And she could see me, too.'

This makes me wonder: If the customer had used his mobile phone to call the reservations clerk while he was standing directly in front of her, *then* would she have seen the absurdity of her ways? And if she did, would she have told her managers about it? Or made a suggestion to change it?

Most likely, not.

Key Learning Point

Frontline staff are taught to follow policies and procedures. Often they are hesitant to 'break the rules'. Yet some rules should be broken, or changed, or at least seriously bent from time to time. Are your staff bound by rules they cannot change? If those rules are outdated or problematic, will they tell you?

Action Steps

Bring your staff together in a mood of irreverent fun for a 'Playful Policy Review'. Do something unusual to set the tone: wear party hats, bring a cake to share, show five minutes of a stand-up comedian on video, put a funny sign in front of the room, or use bright magic markers with flipchart paper on the wall.

Make a list (in advance) of key policies and procedures your staff must work with every day. Go through the list with your staff asking two questions: 'What do *you* like least about this policy (or procedure)?' and 'What do our *customers* find most problematic about this policy?'

Write everything down. Keep the mood light and easy in a spirit of playful review. If you wish, ask a third question: 'How would you change this policy if you could?'

After the meeting, carefully study the list, taking one of two key actions:

1. Modify the policy to eliminate or reduce the friction. If your staff have made good points and reasonable suggestions, implementing those changes will boost efficiency, responsibility and staff morale.

2. If the policy cannot be changed (and there may be good reasons not to: security, credit risk, government requirements, etc.), take the time to explain the rationale of the current system to your staff. Be sure they understand it so well that they can explain it in a positive and convincing manner to someone else. After all, this is exactly what they should do every day – with your customers.

Put some stuffing in the staff suggestion box

Here's how to get your staff suggestion box overflowing with fabulous new ideas.

First, move the program on-line with digital instructions, submissions and replies.

Next, create a quick and easy contest every month. Set short timelines for submission of ideas, offer attractive rewards, and use new criteria for winners every month.

Here are just a few examples:

> 'This month the prize is four tickets to the movies. Three sets of four tickets will be given away. Criterion for the month is "cost savings". How can we reduce expenses while keeping our morale and effectiveness high? Get cost-conscious and submit your best ideas to greatidea@staffsuggestions by July 30. Ideas may be submitted by individuals or by groups. Winners will be announced by e-mail on August 4.'

> 'The prize this month is a one-day external training program on the topic of your choice. Four winners will be chosen. Awards this month are for "quick-wins". What can be done in the company *right now* to make an immediate improvement? Send in your ideas by e-mail by August 30. Winners will be announced on September 3.'

> 'This month the focus is on revenue enhancement. What can we do to increase sales and income? Winning suggestions receive a $100 gift certificate, valid for one year. Three certificates will be awarded. Ideas to be submitted by September 30. Winners will be announced on October 2.'

> 'This month the focus is on improving internal communications. What can we do to increase the quality and quantity of sharing between departments? How can we stimulate constructive dialog for the benefit of all? The prize is a one-year subscription to

the professional magazine of your choice. Five winners will be chosen. Send in your ideas by October 30. Winners will be announced on November 1.'

'Break the mold! This month we want "off the wall" ideas. What quantum innovations should we consider? What "out of the box" ideas can you think of? No suggestions too wild to submit. Prizes awarded for stretching the envelope in completely new directions. Winners get two days off with full pay. Take a long weekend on the company – and keep on thinking! Two winners will be chosen. Submit your ideas by November 30. Winners announced at our staff conference on the same day.'

See how this approach keeps your suggestion program interesting and alive? After a few months, everyone will be talking about winners, prizes and new ideas. Which is exactly what you want!

Key Learning Point

Management no longer has 'all the right answers'. Use a creative staff suggestion program for a steady flow of effective, new ideas.

Action Steps

Liven up your staff suggestion program with new criteria and prizes every month.

Respond to suggestions within one week. Don't make people wait too long for a response from 'The Committee'. Be candid. If the answer is no, say so. If the answer is yes, give an implementation date.

Act upon the best suggestions you receive. Nothing demonstrates your commitment more than staff suggestions recognized, rewarded and immediately put to work.

Are there even more practical ways to improve your organization's suggestion scheme? Sure there are. Got a suggestion?

If we implement them all, you have not succeeded

Singapore is a small country, always looking for new ways to expand, grow and succeed. That requires a constant stream of creative policies and innovative, fresh ideas.

A high-powered panel of financial industry players was convened to help open up the financial sector. Their mission was to propose new ways of stimulating investment and development in the banking, securities, insurance and fund management industries.

The charter to this group was especially open-minded and demanding. At a press conference introducing the panel members, one leading government official said:

'If we implement *all* the recommendations your panel comes up with, then you have not succeeded. You must go further, giving us ideas and suggestions *beyond* what we are ready to implement at this time.'

What a powerful way to ask for – and demand – 'over the horizon' thinking.

Key Learning Point

To keep your culture vibrant and evolving, you must consider ideas that are well beyond what makes sense right now. You must look ahead today, look beyond tomorrow and look 'over the horizon' for the future.

Action Steps

The next time you seek a truly fresh perspective, challenge your team to create proposals beyond what makes sense today. If they offer only practical suggestions you can implement right away, they've failed. If they force you to a higher plane to see what might be in the future, they – and you – have succeeded.

Push into the white space

The world is changing quickly with big rewards for innovators and creators of new value.

When your system says 'no', 'cannot' or 'won't do it', that's a clue to *open up* for new possibilities and new approaches that *add new value*.

Change 'cannot' into 'How can we?' Transform 'no' into 'Let's find a yes.' Convert 'won't do it' into 'How should we make this happen?'

It took days to communicate by mail, so fax machines crossed the divide. But fax machines were bound to a physical location. Now e-mail bridges the gap.

Mothers can't work and be close to their children? Day care in the workplace solved the problem.

Computers were too bulky to carry? Laptops became notebooks then personal digital assistants.

The United States has been upfront as a land of perpetual innovation. 'Do your own thing!' 'If it isn't broken, break it!' 'Build a better mousetrap!' 'Find a better way!' These are keynotes of a culture pushing forward. Think Disneyland, Microsoft, Hollywood, Apple, Wal-Mart, Amazon, Amway, Dell...

Key Learning Point

You don't need to be American or Asian or European to make this work. You just need to be awake, alert and keen to make improvements.

Action Steps

The next time your structure or system says 'no', 'cannot', or 'we don't do it that way', take another look. Think outside the box. Push into the white spaces that surround you. Don't be content just doing it right – find a way to do it better!

Whine, moan and complain – then contribute!

Every month I receive messages from students and readers that begin, 'I got such terrible service from...' and often close, '...and I'll never go back there again!'

I find these stories upsetting, occasionally entertaining, but rarely are they motivating or instructive.

Here's why:

Anyone with enough intelligence and emotion to muster a written complaint also has the ability to offer a constructive solution. If you can see what's *wrong* with a situation, you must have some idea about what would set it *right*.

Noticing problems is *half* the puzzle; getting things improved is the more important part.

If you are upset with a vendor, colleague or business partner, you must have some expectations unmet, some needs ignored or some preferences overlooked.

Your view of the situation is unique and your perspective may be very useful to the other party. Clearly stated, your requests and recommendations could make a difference.

Unless you enjoy complaining for its own sake, follow these five simple steps to help everyone improve.

How to complain for action

1. State your original understanding, including the promise you heard and the standards you expected.

2. Identify the flaw, gap or oversight you experienced.

3. Explain the consequences you have suffered: costs, anxiety, adverse impact.

4. Request specific remedial action and/or compensation.

5. Make a suggestion for improvement. Help the other party do a better job the next time.

Key Learning Point

You have the right to complain when things do not work out as you expected. But complaining is only half the job. You also have a responsibility to contribute.

Action Steps

The next time something goes wrong and you want to 'give someone a piece of your mind', make sure that piece is constructive.

We have a responsibility to the future

The senior management retreat was intended to harness commitment for a new corporate vision. The new vision was big, bold... and essential for success in the rapidly changing world of financial services and solutions.

One senior manager asked if it was necessary to abandon the existing mission statement and core values, which had been nurtured with care for many years.

The president responded with an eloquent statement of corporate (and personal) responsibility. He said:

'We should honor the past, acknowledging the efforts that have brought us to this place and time. We would not be enjoying this success without the dedication, imagination and sacrifices made by those in this room and many others.

'At the same time, we have a responsibility to the future. The world is changing quickly. Customers' needs are evolving more rapidly than ever before. New possibilities and new consequences are unfolding all around us.

'We stand in the present based upon our efforts in the past. Yet we must do what is required to be valuable and relevant in the future. We demonstrate our respect for the past and our commitment to the future by the actions we take here today.'

Key Learning Point

Success should be recognized and rewarded, but not to the point of righteousness, complacency or arrogance. Nostalgia can be a pleasant hobby, but a dangerous vocation.

Action Steps

In which area of your life are you proud of your expertise and achievements? Do you still challenge yourself to improve in that domain? What action can you take today for a more satisfying life tomorrow?

POSITIVE,
PRODUCTIVE PARTNERS

'World-class service is like a best-selling book.
It comes from passionate people, working
together as positive, productive partners.'

Creating partnership agreements

Partnerships are essential in our emerging digital age.

Small players with good partnerships can grab precious market share from larger, established names. Digital commerce rewards innovation and collaboration, not old buildings and traditions.

At the Westin Hotel in Singapore, more than twenty framed certificates hang on the wall announcing 'Partnership Agreements' with key customers and suppliers.

Both parties agree to call upon one another as supplier or vendor of first choice, to provide new and special services to each other before offering them to others, and to do all possible to help build each other's business.

The partnership program is reinforced by continuous dialog, quarterly reviews, a partners' newsletter and other special events. Strong value flows both ways.

Key Learning Point

You can partner with customers, suppliers, even your competitors. Instead of competition, use *co-opetition.* Don't fight over the small pieces. Work together and make a bigger pie.

Action Steps

What are you doing to cultivate exceptional partnerships with your best customers and suppliers? Who can you build a stronger partnership with this month: customers, suppliers, competitors, regulators, peers, employees or bosses? And what about your partnerships at home? The very same principles can apply.

Cross-town collaboration

If you have a problem with your Hewlett Packard or IBM product in Singapore, simply take it to the Post Office and they will forward it to the repair center at no charge.

When it's repaired and ready to collect, the Post Office will return your machine to your home or office, or back to the Post Office location of your choice.

You can even pay for repairs at the point of delivery if they're not covered by the manufacturer's guarantee.

This is a good example of win–win partnership between technology companies and a government agency resulting in better service for customers like you.

Watch for more 'cross-border, cross-town' partnerships between government, commerce, education, medicine, neighborhoods, communities and even spiritual institutions as *everyone* becomes more creative and customer-focused.

Key Learning Point

Old boundaries can become open borders for creative cooperation. If working together produces more convenience or value for the customer, then pursue the new partnership with vigor.

Action Steps

In which industry, agency, association or institution do you work? Which organizations are considered 'outside' of your domain? How might you creatively collaborate on behalf of your common customers? What could you do to surprise your clients? What would raise their eyebrows? What would raise your service?

Are you pulling in the same direction?

I am amazed at the effort companies put into building service brands on the outside, yet how fragmented they can be on the inside.

When fragmentation on the inside is experienced by customers on the outside, real trouble is brewing for the brand.

My student, KP, bought a new notebook computer at his nearby Mega-Mall. He was already brand-loyal – this was his fourth computer in a row from the same company.

The notebook came with automatic one-year coverage. KP paid $1,300 extra for an extended three-year warranty.

Unfortunately, someone smashed the window of his car and stole the new computer within a few months of purchase.

The next day, KP saw the same computer advertised in the newspaper and called the telephone number listed. The company does not sell direct to consumers, but promised to refer his request to an official 'reseller'.

The reseller never called. KP contacted the company again. This time the reseller did call, but was completely unaware of the advertisement in the newspaper. KP explained exactly what he wanted and stressed his urgent need for a new machine. Two days later, the reseller sent him a quote for a completely different and more expensive computer.

KP was now desperate to reconnect and incredibly frustrated by the poor service. He bought a new computer of a different brand...from a different reseller.

What a shame! The computer company lost a lifetime loyal customer due to a weak link in the sales and service chain. I wonder how many other urgent sales leads are lost in this chasm of poor reseller service?

KP then called the company, asking for a refund of his extended three-year service warranty. The computer had been stolen before the warranty started, so the computer company had no financial exposure, no liability, no risk.

The company did not call back for two weeks. KP called again and was told his request had been referred to the Legal Department. Another week passed before the Legal Department replied, 'No refund.'

KP asked to speak to the Legal Department Manager, and was refused. The company sent another notice stating, 'The policy is non-cancellable. No refund.'

What a crying shame! This company took in $1,300 for an extended warranty they will never fulfil from a customer already saddened by the theft of his computer.

What a perfect time to show compassion and flexibility, provide a refund or at least credit towards another product or service. What an ideal moment to restore loyalty to the company. What a terrible time to count on the Legal Department for world-class customer service.

Key Learning Point

Your service reputation is built, or destroyed, in every moment of customer contact. If your marketing, delivery or service partners are weak, *your* reputation is at risk. If one department is out of touch, *your* service image takes the hit. Can you afford to partner with people who do not protect your reputation? Can you allow one department to sabotage your commitment to quality and customer care?

Action Steps

Make a visual map of every business partner you rely upon. Then map each department that makes contact with your customers. Now rank them all from best to worst in quality, flexibility, competence and customer care. Take a hard look at the bottom 25%. These are the weakest links that are likely to offend your customers and colleagues, and do damage to your future.

Don't let it happen. Make the decision now: either bring them up with firm support, or throw the bums right out.

Do 'captive customers' deserve great service?

A government employee questioned whether my service teaching had any value for his department.

After all, he reasoned, why bother giving a high level of service to 'captive customers' who have no choice?

I've got many answers to this loaded question. These three pack a punch:

First, captive customers may have no choice about whether or not to work with an internal department or government agency, but they have plenty of choice about the attitude they bring to the interactions.

The Department of Motor Vehicles in Connecticut, United States has made a profound effort to increase speed of service, upgrade office atmosphere and improve attitudes of the staff.

What's the result? Customers wait in line with appreciation rather than frustration. They speak on the phone with patience instead of displeasure. And they approach the counter with a smile instead of a frown.

Who wins from this effort to upgrade civil service? The customers *and* the staff.

Second, how do government agencies attract and retain good people? It's not by profit sharing, and stock options don't exist.

In government service (and many private organizations) extraordinary staff build long-term careers when the organization is ambitious and attractive. People want to stay when the organization is aiming for better performance, working for better results, making it easier for people to do a good job and feel fulfilled when the job gets done.

This means creating a culture where service is a top priority, where continuous improvement becomes a passion.

Dead organizations collect only dead wood.

Third, I am always surprised when government employees think they have no competition. Don't they understand that every country and city must compete for investment, for tourism, for immigration and retention of best talent, for improving the quality of life?

Where would you rather build your factory, open your regional office, launch or expand your career, or settle and grow your family? Would you prefer somewhere with a dynamic and progressive civil service, or some place with a government bureaucracy that's stuck in the ancient past?

Government employees who think customer service is only for the private sector have their heads buried in the sand. Quicksand.

Key Learning Point

Don't take 'captive customers' for granted. They deserve the best service you can provide. Your payoff may not be in profits, but in the pride and pleasure you give, and receive.

Action Steps

Examine the attitudes and standards you use when serving customers who 'don't have a choice'. Be sure they are up the same level you would apply if your job or career was on the line.

Keep your suppliers eager with a 70/30 split

To keep your suppliers on their toes, try this smart tip I learned from the Group Purchasing Manager of Asia Pacific Breweries.

Whenever he contracts to purchase items from more than one supplier, he gives one vendor 70% of the total purchase, while a second vendor gets 30%. And he tells them both exactly what he is doing.

Why this unequal split? And why tell the two suppliers about it? Here's why:

If the first vendor does a good job, she knows she is keeping well over half the total purchase volume. But if she does a poor job, she knows she stands to lose more than half of what she is currently supplying.

On the other hand, if the second vendor does a great job, he knows he could more than double his orders if he takes over from the first vendor. However, if he does a poor job, he knows he is dispensable as he supplies less than half the company's required volume.

This is an interesting technique for motivating supplier partners that smart purchasing managers understand. Now you know about it, too.

Key Learning Point

Effective programs with your supplier partners help everyone succeed. Be deliberate, and creative, in your contracts.

Action Steps

Identify your most important supplier partners. Review your agreements with them on a regular basis. Be sure they are motivated to give you the best service they can right now, with an eye towards more business in the future.

You're as good as your weakest link

I flew to Fiji from Singapore via Australia, requesting vegetarian meals throughout. But not a single vegetarian dish was provided.

What's unusual is that I checked and rechecked every step of the way: by telephone before departure, at check-in in Singapore, at the First Class Lounge in Sydney, aboard the airplane to Fiji, with airline staff on the ground in Fiji, during check-in at the Fiji airport, and once again in the Lounge in Sydney on the way home.

Every step of the way my special meals were 'confirmed'. I even received boarding passes issued from the airlines with 'VGML' (for 'vegetarian meal') printed in bold.

The strangest experience was the last. As I boarded for the flight from Sydney back to Singapore, I asked the steward about my special meal. He confirmed before take-off, 'Yes, Mr. Kaufman. Strict vegetarian, no eggs, no dairy.'

But during the meal service hours later he came back and said, 'We thought we had the meal on board, but it is not here. Would you mind the chicken or fish?' (I ate the fruit.)

This whole experience was more entertaining than upsetting, but it certainly got me thinking. The travel agent, telephone reservations staff, check-in agent and cabin crew are not 'responsible' for catering on the aircraft. But they do rely upon their partners to deliver.

Key Learning Point

When a customer assesses your business, you are only as good as your weakest link.

Action Steps

Which is the weakest service link in *your* organization? You may think it's not in your department, hence not your problem. Think again.

CREATING SERVICE CULTURE

'The culture of an organization is like the
beauty of a garden, requiring clear vision
...and continuous attention.'

Four steps to a better service culture

If you have the interest and determination to improve the service culture in your organization, or in your life, these four steps will help:

First, your *intention* must be clear. What do you want to do? Make a better product? Delight and keep your customers? Build a more powerful reputation? Create an attractive place to work, or an enlightened place to live? You've got to know where you want to go or you are never going to get there.

Second, your *direction* must be known. Where are you now, compared to where you want to be? If you can't see or admit to the reality of the moment, you can't set a clear direction forward. What should be changed about the way things are? What should be stopped or started? What obstacles and challenges lie ahead? What must be overcome or created?

Third, your *articulation* must be appealing. In words and images we invent ourselves, commit ourselves and align ourselves with others. The language you choose must arouse, persuade, motivate and inspire. Articulate your vision with impeccable care. Every word makes a difference.

Fourth, your *actions* must be deliberate and persistent, guided by the three steps above.

Key Learning Point

You can shape the culture in your company, department or organization. Start with a powerful intention. Know where you want to go. Craft words and images to inspire your team. Take only aligned, consistent actions.

Action Steps

Follow these steps with clarity and passion and watch your service culture grow.

Stop looking for the 'X factor'

Managers ask how to find staff with that 'X factor' for great customer service.

I say stop looking for the X factor. Create it!

The receptionist at Hewlett-Packard smiled and asked how she might help. When I told her who I'd come to see, she gave me a visitor's pass and directions, and a small gift; a packet of 'Post-It Notes' praising HP's recent awards for providing excellent service and support.

I smiled as I accepted the gift. She smiled as she gave it to me. It was a 'win' for me to receive the present, and for her to give it away. It's a big win for HP to have customers and counter staff smiling all day long.

No magic X factor here, just a smart and simple system... implemented with management approval.

I visited the showroom of a European car dealer. Walking to the restroom, I saw a dollar coin on the floor. Stooping down to pick it up, I discovered it was *glued to the floor*.

I stood up and saw the technicians laughing at my expense. I was not the first customer to be caught by their little joke.

What a losing situation! The service technicians show disrespect by laughing at customers every day.

No lack of X factor here, just a stupid situation to embarrass customers...implemented with management consent.

Key Learning Point

Make it easy for staff to share that special X factor. Build smart systems to help source and support it.

Action Steps

Find where your customers may be confused, embarrassed or upset. Fix it. Find where they could be appreciated and delighted. Create it.

Eye-to-eye at the 'Staff Recognition Center'

The Singapore National Eye Center has a unique approach to building customer loyalty and boosting staff morale. In the attractive main lobby, management posts customer compliments in a prominent area called the 'Staff Recognition Center'. Alongside each letter hangs a picture of the staff member cited, and a certificate of appreciation signed by the Managing Director.

Imagine how these staff feel when they come to work each morning. Just walking through the lobby they know they are appreciated – not only by their customers, but also by their organization. Imagine how customers feel when they come for their appointments. They already anticipate receiving good service, and are more likely to express their appreciation when they get it. This is win–win–win at its best: the customer wins, the staff wins, and the National Eye Center wins.

Key Learning Point

You can do this, too! When compliments arrive, be sure to share the news – not just in the staff cafeteria or the in-house newsletter.

Action Steps

Post testimonials (tastefully) in a public place, on your website, or in your regular mailings to customers.

When complaints come in, you can publicize these, too. Be sure to include a response from the organization expressing appreciation for your customer's feedback and stating clearly what's been done to improve the situation.

Chasing chickens builds a better culture

A technology company and major distributor teamed up as business partners to serve the banking market.

But both companies were so proud of their own capabilities and relationships they ended up working *around* each other rather than *with* each other to secure new business.

The head of the distributor finally called his counterpart at the technology company and said, 'I'd rather see our people compete by chasing chickens than get in each other's way chasing the same customers!'

To his surprise, his counterpart declared, 'You're on. Let's do it!'

Two weeks later the sales forces of both companies met on a large open field. One hundred chickens were released and the race to capture 'chicken-share' was on!

Net results: Technology Company – 33 chickens. Major Distributor – 32 chickens. The other 35 chickens escaped.

Everyone got the message. After this exceptional event, both sides worked more closely to capture the total market.

Key Learning Point

Building a culture of partnership takes more than just business agreements. You need to cultivate a *spirit* that brings people together.

Action Steps

What memorable activities of culture-building have you participated in lately? Which do you recall? What episodes of bonding and camaraderie will you create?

How *hot* is our service?

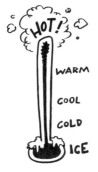

A large bank came to me for the first time seeking a big improvement in their retail counter service. They asked me for 'customer service training' but also complained about the shallow impact of classroom training efforts from other providers. I was hesitant. Classroom training is only a partial solution, especially for a high-traffic, face-to-face service environment. To make it more effective, creativity is needed. So I invented a novel approach involving customers and staff, immediate feedback, and clear targets and objectives. Perhaps you can use this, too.

1. Set up a large colorful 'Service Quality Thermometer' in the lobby. Place it where customers can use it easily.

2. Place three 'voting buttons' next to the thermometer labeled 'Good service', 'Service OK' and 'Service needs improvement'.

3. Each time the first button is touched, a light cheery sound emerges and the thermometer goes 'up' a notch. When the 'Service OK' button is touched, the nice sound is heard but the thermometer remains the same. The button marked 'Service needs improvement' makes no sound, but the thermometer drops a notch.

4. At the end of each day, post the results on an attractive monthly scoreboard marked: 'How *hot* is our service?' Locate the scoreboard in full view of both customers and staff.

5. Over time, a standard will emerge for each branch of the bank. Gradually raise the standard. Run contests between the branches. Give 'pat on the back' recognition. Highlight past performance and illustrate 'Our target for today!'

6. Ask customers who touch 'Service needs improvement' for their immediate recommendations and feedback. Ask

those who touch 'Good service' what key elements of the interaction had satisfied their needs.

7. Based upon this genuine and immediate feedback, design a training program to help staff understand and deliver what really works.

Key Learning Point

Excellent service quality training *is* important, and sometimes a classroom is the best place to provide it. But training should be always supported by a work environment that generates interest and participation.

Action Steps

Back up your training efforts with creative programs to involve staff, and customers, in a continuous journey towards service improvement. Use the 'Service Quality Thermometer' idea, or come up with creative plans of your own. Creativity + Training = Results.

The 'friendliest airport in the world'

Singapore's Changi Airport has been rated #1 in the world so many times the trophy cabinet is bulging.

They've hit #1 in efficiency, speed, shopping, security, safety and ease of use.

But the category called 'courtesy and friendliness' has eluded Changi Airport's capture. This is not surprising, perhaps, given that the local culture has grown in a city known more for 'trading and exchanging' than 'providing gracious warmth and hospitality'.

Now the airport is facing this challenge head-on. The depth and magnitude of commitment are impressive: a brand new 'service promise' with high impact launch program for 7,000 staff, customized full-day training for 3,000 front-line staff members, monthly courtesy awards, customer feedback kiosks, service improvement contests, mystery traveler audits, constant reminders for staff (and customers) with posters, badges and banners, newsletter articles, special announcements and more.

This is total commitment, typical of Singapore Changi Airport. With such intensity and clarity of focus, the program will surely work.

Key Learning Point

Changing a culture takes time and effort, energy, creativity and focus. It's not a project to do halfway, not for the half-hearted.

Action Steps

What upgrade or improvements are *you* working on right now? Are you doing *everything you can* to really make it happen? Need some inspiration? Come visit Singapore's Changi Airport.

Driving home the culture of honesty

I accompanied a visiting friend from my apartment in Singapore to a taxi waiting downstairs.

He climbed into the back seat and promptly sat on a wallet left behind by the previous passenger.

My friend looked inside the wallet and found money, credit cards and personal identification. I suggested taking the wallet upstairs right away to call the owner. The taxi driver allowed me to copy down the necessary information...but he wouldn't let the wallet out of his sight.

He did not speak English well, but he made his message very clear. 'My duty,' he gestured to explain. 'She left wallet in my taxi. I must report to company right away. Then *I* must return the wallet!'

This culture of honesty and personal responsibility deserves an honorable mention. Every year Singapore taxi drivers return hundreds of books, wallets and packages accidentally left behind by passengers.

The drivers consider it a matter of honor to return the items in person. Taxi companies consider it a commendable action and duly note the deed in a driver's permanent record.

Bravo for the culture surrounding, and supporting, the taxi drivers of Singapore.

Key Learning Point

When a culture is strong and supported, individual behavior naturally aligns with the intention and commitment of the group.

Action Steps

What can you do to promote a strong culture? What actions should you take, and what traditions should you reinforce, to strengthen your culture and your values?

The Police Debates

When a senior officer of the Singapore Police Force (SPF) asked for my opinion about service improvement, mindset training and new technology, I became curious.

I did some detective work of my own and discovered the SPF holds *internal debates* on provocative service questions. It's one of the best ideas I've seen for developing a service culture. Here's how they did it. You can do it, too!

The debate competition is open to all. Sixteen teams of three compete in a preliminary round. A ballot system determines the teams' order of appearance, motions to be debated and position (proposition or opposition) each team will take. The winning team of each pair advances to the next round. Competition continues until two teams reach the finals.

A judging panel includes police reservists in the private sector and other specialists in quality service training.

The judging criteria are as follows:
- Substance of speech – 35%
- Organization of speech – 25%
- Rebuttal / reply to floor – 10%
- Teamwork – 10%
- Diction – 10%
- Showmanship – 10%

Motions for debate in the preliminary round:
- Improving service makes customers more demanding.
- High service standards increase work competency.
- Lack of training is the cause for service lapses.

Motions for debate in the quarterfinals:
- Striving for service excellence compromises SPF's image as an enforcement agency.
- The nature of police work does not allow officers to provide quality service.
- It is more important for SPF to be results-oriented than service-oriented.

Motions for debate in the semifinals:

- To provide quality service, SPF should rely more on new technology.
- To provide quality service, only experienced staff should be placed in frontline work.

Motion for debate in the finals:

- To achieve service excellence, an officer's attitude matters more than their training.

The competition results were impressive. The original intention was to increase staff involvement in the annual campaign, stimulate interest in the subject of quality service, create better understanding about the importance of key service issues, help management understand staff concerns about being service-oriented and learn about any implementation difficulties that may have been overlooked.

In the words of the SPF: 'All of these benefits were achieved. Staff were very forthcoming with their opinions and the activity was one of the favorites among officers so far. Demand to enter the competition exceeded supply.'

Key Learning Point

In today's world of intensifying competition and rising customer expectations, organizations need staff who understand key issues and appreciate sometimes conflicting points of view.

Action Steps

What questions about service, innovation and teamwork do you want your staff to thoroughly and thoughtfully consider?

Make a list of important issues everyone in your organization should understand. Draft them into 'position statements' that can be debated 'for' and 'against'. Set up a competition with teams, judges and high profile presentations. Then watch your people kick into action with creative energy, full participation and a constructive new flow of ideas, insights and inspiration.

A rising tide lifts all boats – except those that sink!

Clients often ask me how to motivate stodgy 'old-timers' to give better service, work more effectively on teams or contribute to building a stronger learning culture. One company even asked me to help 'crack four tough nuts' out of a staff strength of over five hundred!

My response to these situations is this: stop spending so much time and energy trying to convert the few who are 'stuck in the mud' and unwilling to change. Instead, put more focus and attention on staff who *do* want to learn, *are* willing to change and *will* improve their skills.

Over time, the 'old timers' will become uncomfortable with all the focused and positive efforts. They will wake up and get with the program, or leave.

Please note: I am not saying that 'old-timers' are always a problem. Their wisdom and experience can be a precious asset. But in today's fast moving world, *everyone* must be willing to learn, ready to change and eager to grow. If someone refuses to rise with the tide, let them sink.

Key Learning Point

Don't let a few stodgy characters from the 'old school' keep you from building an effective learning organization.

Action Steps

To keep your culture vibrant and growing strong: conduct more training, launch new campaigns, circulate interesting articles, share real stories, run frequent contests, reward staff initiatives, give plenty of praise, share benchmarking results, capture and communicate up-to-date customer information. Do *everything* positive you possibly can. And then do even more.

No news is...bad news!

 Many companies treat customer service as a necessary evil, an afterthought, only needed if mistakes and problems arise. This viewpoint is best reflected in the antiquated mindset: 'No news is good news!'

When it comes to customers, that's bad news! Here's why:

If you have a customer who is happy and you do not give them a chance to tell you, you lose one of the strongest opportunities to increase customer loyalty. The need to be internally consistent is a driving force in shaping future behavior. In other words, if customers tell you how and why they are happy, they are very likely to repeat the behavior that caused them such satisfaction – which was doing business with you!

And what if you have a customer who is not happy? Who would you rather they tell all about it – you, or your prospects, competitors and other customers?

Key Learning Point

Theodore Levitt said it best: 'One of the surest signs of a bad or declining relationship with a customer is the absence of complaints (or compliments!). Nobody is ever that satisfied, especially over an extended period of time. The customer is either not being candid, or is not being contacted.'

Action Steps

Contact a number of your recent customers right away. Ask them for immediate feedback on your service. If they are happy, your call will make them happier. If they are not completely happy, your call will give you a precious opportunity to make it so.

Complaints + compliments = good communication

Some companies track a monthly 'complaints and compliments ratio' for each branch, store, department, country or station. This approach has a fundamental flaw. Here's why:

A complaints and compliments ratio encourages staff to actively avoid or suppress written complaints from customers. After all, every written complaint will impact the ratio to their disadvantage.

For example, if your station gets 3 compliments and 0 complaints, and my station has 6 compliments and 3 complaints, whose station has a better ratio? Yours has, of course.

But which station is gathering more written feedback from customers? Which station is harnessing more input, suggestions, responses and reactions for detailed review? Mine!

I agree that staff should do whatever they can to satisfy customers right away, but they should also *encourage* customers to write down and submit their comments quickly and easily.

This real-time 'voice of the customer' feedback should be circulated widely within the organization and carefully studied by all departments. Such direct input can provide valuable insights and better understanding of currrent, and changing, customer expectations.

When comments filtered through managers replace direct commentary written by customers, subtle nuances may be lost. Don't let this happen to you.

Instead of a complaints and compliments ratio, try using a 'comments from customers ratio'. With this approach, gathering bountiful customer input is more important – and rewarded – than suppressing customer complaints.

*Key Learning Point

Written feedback from customers is priceless. It gives you unvarnished input you can study, circulate and discuss. Instead of penalizing your staff for complaints, praise them for actively seeking input and ideas from the folks who know you best – your customers.

Action Steps

Design a small, attractive Customer Comment Card that is simple and easy to use. On one side print 'Thank you for letting us know' with a blank area for their comments. On the other side, provide space for your customer's name and contact information (optional).

Place the cards where customers will easily find them: on counters, in packaging, etc. Give cards to all staff members and encourage them to seek out customers' comments.

Track the volume of written input over time. Run a contest to increase the flow. Set a standard for the minimum number of customer comments each month.

8 ways to get close to your customer

Want to add more value to your customers? Be sure you know what to add!

Here are eight proven ways to get close to your customers and find out what they value, what they care about, what they *really* want:

1. *Ask them!* Whether in print, in person or over the phone, nothing beats asking customers exactly what they want, and how they want it. (Ask them what they don't want, too!) Use printed sheets, mail-back forms, comment cards, telephone scripts and more.

2. *Conduct focus groups.* Bring a group of customers together for an open-ended chat session. Set them at ease and get them talking about what they really like, don't like and wish they could get from your business. Don't defend, justify or argue. Just ask questions and take good notes. Follow up with a sincere and generous 'Thank you!'

3. *Study complaints and compliments.* Every message from a customer brings value to your doorstep. Compliments show you what to reinforce. Complaints point to new ideas and action steps for improvement.

4. *Set up a customer hotline.* Some customers will tell you what they think, but they want an 'anonymous' way to do it. Fine! Set up a special voice recording 'hotline' for customers only. And don't worry about receiving any strange messages; just sort through them for the gems!

5. *Hire a Mystery Shopper.* Have someone you trust mingle with your customers and strike up conversation to find out what they do and do not like.

6. *Become a customer of your best competitors.* Use all their products and services, and compare them to your own. Ask their Customer Service Center to describe all the services available in detail. Then copy the best and do better than the rest.

7. *Visit your customer's site.* Go to your customer's physical location to see exactly how they put your products and services to use. See with your own eyes what works and what doesn't, what gets used all the time and what gets left behind.

8. *Go online to seek more feedback.* Find an Internet user's group related to your industry or topic. Read the postings for new ideas and information. Participate in the discussions. Follow up by e-mail to gain even deeper input and understanding.

What is *your* favorite technique for getting close to the customer?

Key Learning Point

Before you invest time, money and effort into 'adding value' for your customers, make sure you know exactly what value to add!

Action Steps

Stay close to your customers throughout the year with a robust program of connection and consultation. Your customers will appreciate the contact, your staff will learn from the contents, and your business will grow from the continuous, constructive communication.

Develop a yearning for learning

Want to learn something and deepen your relationship with others at the same time? Here's an easy way to do it:

1. Choose a book or current article you want to read and study.

2. Select the people with whom you'd enjoy discussing this text. This works well with one or two, or with an entire company or department. The dynamics are different, but the benefits can be equally strong.

3. Send copies of the book or article to your chosen 'learning partners' with an invitation to read and discuss the text together.

4. Reading a text is already a conversation between you and the author(s), but the conversation can be somewhat one-sided. Reading and discussing with others deepens your learning in very valuable ways.

5. Start with something short and easy to read, one article or chapter at a time. Go slowly enough to get value from your conversations, but quickly enough to keep your learning partners engaged.

6. Before you read, discuss these questions together:

   Why did you choose this text? What benefits do you anticipate from your reading and discussions?

   Why did you choose these partners? What interests and concerns do you currently have or share in this area?

   What do you anticipate the author will say in this text? What do you already know about this area?

   What are your current ideas about this area of your life? Are you a beginner looking for a good introduction? Or are you already strong in this domain, and looking to fine-tune your understanding or upgrade your performance?

7. During and after your reading of the text, discuss these questions together:

What opinions did the author express? Remember, just because it is in print doesn't mean it is necessarily 'true'.

What distinctions and examples does the author use to make his or her case?

Where do you agree with the author? disagree?

In what way are your current actions consistent with the author's beliefs? In what ways do they differ?

What new actions can you take that will be useful for you or others? What benefits do you anticipate?

How has your understanding of this area changed? Have you strengthened your opinions? enriched your understanding? changed your position on any important issues?

How will you and your learning partners extend this conversation? What other text would you like to read together?

Key Learning Point

Reading together is a great way to share new learning and improve your understanding, your work and your life.

I learned this valuable method of reading and learning with partners during my post-graduate participation in the *Ontological Design Course*, a life-enriching innovation created by Dr. Fernando Flores.

Action Steps

Learn something new and valuable this month. Choose a text, choose some partners and get going.

Use the list of questions on these pages to guide your thinking and learning together. Enjoy the conversations!

PERSONAL AND PROACTIVE

'Getting your service in shape takes commitment.
It's hard work, but the results feel great!'

Positive, proactive communication

Every insurance company in the world is concerned about 'persistency', keeping policies in force by making sure clients pay their premiums year after year.

A small increase in persistency can yield a very large boost in company profits.

I have policies with several insurance companies. Every year I am stunned by the incredibly impersonal notices I receive stating: 'Premium Due'.

These communications seem to regard me as nothing more than an account number, a payment amount and a due date. As a prospect, I was engaged as a real person with needs and concerns, hopes and dreams. I was treated as a valued partner in the necessary world of personal financial planning.

Now that the policy is in force, I am just an invoice.

Here's what I would much prefer. (If you have an insurance policy, you might appreciate it, too.)

Ten months into the year, two months *before* the premium is due, a smart insurance company should send me a simple customized letter. Something like this:

Dear Mr. Kaufman,

In two months the annual premium for your insurance policy number 123456 will be due.

I want to take a moment now to congratulate you on your decision to keep this policy in force, and to remind you of the many benefits you have been receiving, and will continue to receive, throughout the year.

In addition to basic financial protection for you and your family members, your insurance policy has provided you with (include all of the following that apply):

- *a guaranteed savings program*
- *effective retirement planning*
- *education planning for your children*
- *risk coverage against death or disability, and*
- *precious peace of mind.*

Each year at this time, we ask valued clients like you if any major changes have occurred during the past ten months.

Have you added a new family member? Have you received a promotion or otherwise increased your income? Have you purchased a new home or automobile? Have any of your family members or friends recently married?

If any of these changes have occurred, we encourage you to speak with your insurance agent (name here), who can be easily contacted at (contact details here).

Once again, we congratulate you for maintaining the benefits of your valuable insurance program. If you have any questions, please feel free to contact your agent, or our office directly at (contact details here).

With best regards,

(Fill in the blank with the name of a smart, positive, proactive and profitable insurance company.)

Key Learning Point

Whether you are in education, marketing, retail, logistics, government service, entertainment or insurance, communicating positively and proactively with your clients makes sense.

Action Steps

Don't wait until the last minute. Make an effort to stay in touch with your customers and clients with positive news and proactive views.

Make it person-to-person

Automation is essential for expanding and accelerating service in many industries. But when individual care or attention is required, customers need contact with real people. When human energy flows and connects, good things (can) get done.

Try this experiment:

Call the main number of four companies and state, 'I am calling with a question about your product'. Then ask a few basic questions and rate the quality of service you receive.

Now call four different companies and ask for help again. But this time, make a 'personal connection' first.

Start by saying, 'Hello, I am calling about one of your products. I am hoping you can help me.' (Pause and wait for a reply.) 'You can help? Oh, that's great. Thank you very much. I really appreciate it. My name is (give your full name). Who am I speaking with, please?'

Once again, rate the quality of service you receive. I'll bet the service you get from the second group of calls is friendlier, more thorough and uplifting for you – and for the service provider.

Key Learning Point

When service between companies and customers is provided person-to-person, do everything you can to create, support and enhance a real connection between real people.

Action Steps

1. On the telephone, teach your staff to initiate the personal connection by offering their names. 'Hello. This is Janice Lee in the Accounts Department. How may I help you?'

2. Ask customers politely for their names and how they prefer to be addressed. Then use your customer's name in a friendly tone throughout the service conversation.

3. Provide staff with attractive name tags to wear at work. These may be colorful or elegant, with full name, first name or nickname, as appropriate for your organization.

4. Post complimentary pictures of your staff on the wall in the customer service area. This will help customers 'connect' with the members of your team. Your staff feel proud of themselves and the company if they look good in the photos, so take the time to do this right. Help your staff look and feel their best. Provide good lighting, a good photographer and make-up. Be sure your staff are well dressed, well groomed and smiling!

5. Give staff members personalized business cards to share with their customers. For many frontline employees, this small step dramatically increases pride in, and ownership of, their service. If you have a large number of frontline or temporary staff, create a standard business card that can be easily customized with a nicely handwritten or computer-printed name.

6. Help your staff connect with real customers by hosting frequent focus groups. Invite your customers 'inside' to meet your staff for regular discussions and brainstorming about your service.

7. Post actual letters of compliments (and complaints) in the staff lounge or cafeteria. Print them in your newsletter with replies and follow-up communications.

8. Videotape customers speaking directly to the camera about your company's service. Edit the tape to use in staff orientation, training sessions, management meetings – even to show at the company dinner and dance. Customer compliments are powerful motivators for excellent service. Genuine complaints can be a wake-up call to improve.

To build your business, appreciate the customers you already have

Consumer banking is a very competitive industry. Banks battle for market share with advertising, free gifts, lower charges, higher interest rates and more.

So much energy and expense are spent attracting new business. But so little effort is invested in truly appreciating the customers they already have.

For example, have you ever bought a house with a housing loan? After you moved in, did the bank call to ask about your new home, or send you a housewarming gift?

Have you ever purchased a car with a car loan? Did the bank send you a note afterwards to congratulate you on your new car, or send you a friendly coupon for a free car wash and wax?

Do you have a credit card? Does your bank ever call you just to say 'Thank you' for using the card and ask if you are happy with the bank's service?

At a bankers' convention I asked if anyone in the audience of 3,000 routinely called their customers just to say 'Thank you!' The answer, predictably, was 'No'.

The bankers were stunned by their own admission.

'Relax,' I said. 'None of the other bankers here are doing it either...not yet.'

Most banking customers have accounts at more than one bank. You probably do too.

What would it take to get you to consolidate most of your banking activity to *one* bank? A free gift, slightly lower charges, or a higher rate of interest?

Not likely. Those incentives exist today and you still have multiple banking accounts.

But if one bank started genuinely thanking you, calling you, truly listening to your thoughts and suggestions about their banking service, would you be more inclined to rely on that bank in the future? to use them again and again? to migrate your accounts to that *one bank* for more comprehensive service?

What would it cost the bank to make those telephone calls to you? Not much. What might it earn the bank? A lot.

Key Learning Point

Picking up new business is important, but it can cost a lot in advertising, special discounts, promotions and new customer orientation. Increasing your business with *existing* customers magnifies the loyalty of those you already have, and substantially boosts your profits.

Action Steps

Pick up the telephone. Write a letter. Send out a few 'free gifts' – not to the new customer you've just signed up, but also to the loyal customers who have been with you all along.

How to pay a powerful compliment

I received a powerful testimonial from a client. I often receive nice letters after my presentations, but this note stood out as exceptionally genuine, specific and sincere. I read it twice, and that got me thinking.

I write 'Thank you' notes every week to colleagues, suppliers and friends. Perhaps you do, too. But how many of my notes – or yours – pack such a positive punch?

I thought, 'If I am going to take the time to send a note, why not write one that really stands out?'

So I studied my client's message again and found four distinct elements working closely together:

1. Acknowledge the high level of *quality* received.

2. Report the *impact* this quality had on the people.

3. Explain how the experience *exceeded* expectations.

4. Gesture towards positive interactions in the *future*.

This formula is simple yet powerful. I used it to compliment a scuba-diving resort I visited for a week. Here's my letter. It took two minutes to write.

Dear Kungkungan Bay Resort,

I want to thank you for a terrific diving vacation last month. The entire resort is a credit to 'environmental tourism' for scuba-diving and for the region.

My friend and I returned home with nothing but positive comments and stories.

We knew the diving would be great, with unusual creatures seen at each location. But we had no idea such great scuba-diving would be coupled with delightful rooms, friendly staff and first-class dining that ranks *way* beyond our expectations.

We will certainly tell our friends about you, and look forward to returning soon.

Sincerely,

Ron Kaufman

Can you see how the simple four-step formula makes this letter so *real* and so effective? Isn't that what you want to do when you send out a letter of compliment or thanks? Now you can do it, in just four easy steps.

Key Learning Point

Sincere compliments motivate, encourage and inspire. The next time *you* praise a deserving person or organization, create a compliment with positive power.

Action Steps

Choose an individual who deserves praise for his or her service skill, energy or commitment. Choose an organization deserving of praise for its plans, purpose or projects. Then use this outline to create compliments everyone will appreciate and remember.

Flexibility slakes a thirst

Graham Harvey, author of *Seducing the Vigilante Customer*, told me this story of a general store owner who followed government policy 'creatively' to solve a problem, close a sale and create a satisfied, repeat customer.

'We arrived on a Sunday morning after a long flight and decided a nice cold beer would be in order. The only problem was, beer was not available for sale on Sundays, even though it was on the shelves at the local general store.

'The solution? We combined ingenuity, flexibility (and thirst!) with friendly customer service.

'"Would it be okay if we took the beer now, but paid for it tomorrow (Monday)?", we asked.

'The store owner thought, and smiled. Problem solved.'

Graham continued, 'As we were staying in self-contained apartments nearby, this was the first of many purchases made at the same store during the week. Result? Happy customers, and healthy profits.'

Key Learning Point

Flexibility is a virtue in dance, life and service. Bending the rules is not the same as breaking them. When people are willing to serve, policies can often be 'adjusted'.

Action Steps

Where can you bend the rules on your customer's behalf without breaking important regulations? Discuss this with your staff, then empower them to act with creativity, flexibility and authority.

Peach pie with your scuba-dive?

Carole is a full-time employee, part-time photographer and an all-time scuba-diving fanatic. She moonlights on weekends with group charters under the sea.

Carole is also a keen advocate of superior customer service, both at work and in her hobby. She wrote:

'I decided to apply what you taught about surprisingly good service to our boat charter business.

'After a full day of diving, everyone was blown away when I brought out a homemade peach pie. Not so much by the taste of the pie (though it was good) but by the unique idea and the effort.

'Needless to say, we have already received referrals and repeat business.'

I'm a scuba-diver, too, with hundreds of dives logged from boats all over the world. But no one, anywhere, has come close to surprising me with a peach pie back on the surface.

Key Learning Point

Special efforts to surprise your customers lead to great memories...and great referrals.

Action Steps

What can you do to delight *your* customers with a surprising touch of pleasure? A photograph? A telephone call? A personal note? Peach pie, anyone?

If not this time, perhaps later

Ever worked hard on a proposal and *not* been awarded the contract? When it happens to me, I say 'Thank you'. My follow-up notes read like this:

'Thank you for the opportunity to get to know you better and offer my services to you. I hope we have a chance to work together in the future. In the meantime, I wish you the best of success. Feel free to contact me when I may be of assistance.'

This note creates good feelings for everyone. The prospect may contact me in the future. If someone else asks about me, he may give a positive comment or an active referral.

Consider the different reactions in these two examples.

I interviewed a consultant but decided not to hire her at this time. She went totally silent, no longer responding to my messages. I wonder if she felt I owed her the business since we met once to discuss it? Or that I should not have chosen another consultant, or could not simply change my mind?

This short-term reaction can have a long-term impact. I often refer people within my business network. Her cordial reply would have secured my positive word of mouth.

I met twice with a financial planner, but made a decision not to use his services. He called me to explore my reasons and accepted them with grace. He asked if he could stay in touch in the future. I gladly agreed. He asked me for referrals when appropriate, which I also agreed to do.

Key Learning Point

Your prospect may become your client in the future, and influence your reputation in the present.

Action Steps

When you make a proposal and you don't get the business, make an *extra* effort to leave a positive impression at the end.

The other guy has a better deal

Have you ever referred a customer somewhere else because you knew they could get a better deal? Sounds crazy, but makes good business sense.

I conducted full-day workshops on 'Achieving Superior Service' in two cities in the Middle East.

The organizer in one city charged a lower fee than the organizer in another. There were differences in the date, location, meals and materials provided, but the workshop content was the same.

Each organizer sent out their own brochure to their own client mailing lists. It happened that several clients in one city signed up for the higher priced event in the other city.

Before accepting these enrollments, the organizer personally called the affected clients to inform them of the lower priced and more conveniently located option.

The organizer 'lost' 12 enrollments (almost $5,000), but *gained* a new level of credibility and respect from his clients, his industry colleagues (competitors), and from me.

'This is one phone call I will never forget,' said one surprised client. 'I will be their customer forever.'

Key Learning Point

If you can help a customer more by sending them to someone else, don't focus on the short-term sale. Take a longer-term view.

Action Steps

The next time your client wants something they could easily get *better* or *cheaper* somewhere else, don't hide it – provide it! The short-term impact may be loss of a single sale, but the long-term result will be increased respect and credibility for you.

Meet Elvis, King of the Road

I had an amazing experience in a brand-new, all-white Mercedes taxi. But it wasn't the car that impressed me – it was the driver.

Martin Lim picked me up in his spotless taxi with current magazines in the back, a selection of CD music, a mobile telephone for my use, digital video TV and an Internet-linked palmtop computer mounted on the dashboard. Lim maintains a database of his regular customers and even sends 'Thank You' notes by e-mail after the ride.

By the time we reached my destination, I didn't want to get out of the car.

Does all this investment pay off? Lim makes *four times* what an average taxi driver makes in his city. But then he isn't a taxi driver. His (self appointed) title is 'Provider of Personalized Limousine Service'.

He even has a nickname – 'Elvis'. The name was given by a former customer, and it sticks. After months of loyal taxi travel, this customer bought a car. But he kept Lim's contact information handy.

Now, whenever the former customer finds himself lost on city streets, he calls Lim on the mobile phone and says, 'You're the King of the Road! Can you help me figure out where I am, and how to get to where I'm going?'

Key Learning Point

Elvis stood out from the crowd by doing things more, better and different from the rest. He wasn't just a singer. He was the King. You can be, too.

Action Steps

Study what everyone else is doing in your business, and then do something else. Make an extra effort. Get busy. Get famous. Get rich.

9

SETTING THE PACE, LEADING THE RACE

'Staying ahead of rising customer expectations requires
continuous effort, innovation and teamwork.'

What is 'Legendary Service'?

Legendary Service.

Many organizations use this phrase to describe and promote their service. But how many have really earned it?

If you give good service, that's not legendary. If you go out of your way for someone, that's not legendary either. But if you provide service *unsurpassed* in your field, that can be legendary service.

Many years ago I lived in the northeastern United States: cold winters, lots of snow, great skiing. I bought a pair of silk long underpants by mail order from a company called L.L. Bean. The silk was smooth and comfortable, the underpants nice and warm.

Then I moved, and moved again, and again. I found myself 20 years later unpacking boxes of clothing in Singapore. There were the old silk underpants.

They were not much use to me now, living near the equator. And even less attractive because they had holes in the knees and were fraying at the ends.

I almost threw them away, then remembered that L.L. Bean features a 'lifetime guarantee'.

I put the underpants in a plain, brown envelope and inserted a simple handwritten note: 'Please replace these.'

I didn't have the company's full address. I had not ordered clothing from them for years. On the outside of the envelope I wrote: L.L. Bean, Customer Service, Maine, USA.

At the post office I felt foolish mailing back such a ragged piece of clothing. It didn't seem right to send old underpants all the way around the world by *airmail*. So for a dollar I sent them the slow way, by sea.

Time passed and I forgot all about it. Life quickly filled with new sports, new clothing, and new underpants.

Two months later an envelope arrived from L.L. Bean. Inside was a money order for one dollar. No explanation, just a dollar. I figured they evaluated the old clothing and calculated its leftover value! I laughed and forgot about it.

Another month passed and a bigger envelope arrived. Inside was a brand new pair of silk long underpants. Same size and color as the old ones, but brand new!

In time, new catalogs arrived from L.L. Bean and I bought some new clothes. I always feel safe buying from them. I know from experience their 'lifetime guarantee' is real.

Months later I was in the United States and called to place a holiday order for some relatives. Chatting with the L.L. Bean telephone representative, I told her the story of returning my old underpants.

'One thing still confuses me,' I confessed. 'What was the one dollar money order for?'

Laughing, she replied, 'Before replacing your underpants, we refunded your postage!'

Twenty-year-old underpants, gladly replaced, including refund of the postage. That's extraordinary. That's truly amazing. *That* is Legendary Service.

Key Learning Point

Using the words 'legendary service' is not enough to make it real. You must expand, imagine, innovate – and *take* real legendary action.

Action Steps

A legend is a story people talk about with admiration and praise, recounting some great deed done in the service of others.

What great deed can you do for customers that is admirable, praiseworthy and *truly unsurpassed*?

Federal Express sets a benchmark

 Whenever I call Federal Express to arrange an outgoing shipment of Ron Kaufman books, tapes, videos and learning resources, FedEx already knows my name, address and account number...even before I tell them who is calling.

FedEx has linked 'inbound caller identification' to their customer database. With this powerful combination, they *do* know who is calling...before they answer the phone.

What impresses me most is that FedEx remembers any *new* telephone numbers I call from and automatically updates its database. Now they know it's me whether I call from my office, home or mobile phone.

It's just a small touch, but it's *nice* (and very convenient) to hear FedEx say 'Good morning, Mr. Kaufman. Are you calling to arrange a shipment from 50 Bayshore Park?'

Compare this with the telephone service from my favorite airline and taxi companies. When I call to make a reservation, they ask for my account or priority number each and every time.

Fair enough, they don't have inbound caller identification and they want a quick way of knowing who I am.

But every time I call, they ask for my telephone number, too. Don't they keep that essential information in their records?

Finally, I asked. The airline and taxi database systems do provide access to all my information (including telephone numbers), but that data is 'two screens away' from the first screen presented to the reservations agent.

So it's simply easier for them to ask for the same basic information from me each and everytime. Easier for them – not for me.

Key Learning Point

Service improvements in one industry soon impact customer expectations in another. The service I get from FedEx influences what I expect from airline and taxi companies.

This transfer of expectations is true in many dimensions of service, including accessibility, after-sales service, ordering and payment flexibility, service recovery policies, upgrade procedures and more.

Question: Which came first: drive-through banking or drive-through restaurants?

My answer: Who cares? They are both common, and expected, today.

Action Steps

If you want to be on the leading edge of customer service and customer expectations, look *beyond* your own industry, beyond what you and your competitors are doing, beyond the obvious 'next step'.

To keep your business out in front, you must benchmark yourself against the best in every industry…and throughout the world.

Education is the star at Starbucks

I avoided caffeine for many years. But with so many flights and late, late nights, I recently tried 'just a sip'. The next day I dunked a Danish pastry. A few days later I asked for 'half a cup, please'. In very little time, I was enjoying café latte for breakfast!

Much has changed in the world of coffee in the past few years. Waiters used to ask, 'Would you like cream with your coffee? Will that be one sugar or two?' Now baristas enquire 'Cappuccino wet or dry? Solo, doppio, soy, low-fat, not-too-hot, extra-hot, full or half-pump mocha?' The menu can be overwhelming.

Except at Starbucks. Starbucks is an extraordinary example of a company with loyal customers and vigorous global growth. One reason is their devotion to quality service. Another is their fanatical commitment to cultivating customers through attractive and persistent *education*.

With my latest café latte I took a copy of each brochure sitting on the counter. Here's the rundown of what you can get simply by taking what's freely offered:

1. The Story of Good Coffee – 12 panels detail the growing cycle, roasting, color and freshness of beans. Eight levels of roasting explained with clear graphics and text. It takes 4,000 beans to make one pound of coffee. The coffee bush takes five years before it yields a single crop.

2. The World of Coffee – another 12-panel tutorial on bean varieties around the world, including descriptions of 24 popular beans in four 'coffee categories' for your tasting pleasure. Also a primer on 'The Four Fundamentals of Brewing'. Ninety percent of your tasting ability is based upon your sense of smell. Ten grams of coffee and 180 millilitres of water is the 'classic recipe' for a great cup of coffee.

3. Espresso. What You Need to Know – I didn't know what I didn't know! Eight panels on 'Grind, Dose, Tamp and

Rate of Pour' with additional insights and graphics on properly steaming milk. The ideal temperature for steamed milk is 66–76 degrees centigrade. Foamed milk is a few degrees cooler due to 'incorporated air'.

4. Experience the Perfect Cup – an 8-panel treatise with cut-away schematics revealing the ingredients and precise architecture of the five most popular drinks. It includes company history and a sidebar on 'additional choices'.

5. Try One, Try Them All – a 2-panel flyer encouraging you to try Starbucks new iced drinks – three unique blends in eleven different flavors.

6. How Are We Doing? – a 4-panel customer survey form with postage paid to return your comments to the waiting eyes and ears at Starbucks.

Starbucks understands. They are not just selling coffee. They are educating and creating loyal customers, building a long-term clientele, increasing understanding while promoting the industry, the products and the brand. This company knows the power of attraction is not just in the drinks, it's in the experience they create – and the rich, steamy, full-bodied *education* they provide.

Key Learning Point

Education adds value, and your customers want a full cup.

Action Steps

What lengths do you go to effectively educate your customers and colleagues? Is your effort a watery dose of weak support with lukewarm staff and systems? Or are you serving a hot, fresh brew of potent answers, proactive ideas and positive, powerful insights?

Now take your team to Starbucks. Order a round of delicious drinks and then get to work. Find a way to match Starbucks' blend of attractive and effective *education*.

My new hat makes me information rich!

I bought a new hat to shield my balding head from the summer sun. The store had over 200 hats, but only one hat offered as much information as protection. My new 'Tilley Hat' cost me plenty. It was worth every cent.

What other hat comes with a four-page Owner's Manual complete with illustrations, explanations and detailed instructions on how to wear it, tie it, wash it and stretch it back to shape? What other hat comes with history, legends and lore all provided?

What other hat explains inside that the cloth is '100% USA cotton duck', the fittings 'British brass' and the sewing done with 'Canadian persnicketiness'?

What other hat comes with a life-long guarantee against destruction or loss and the directive (I'm not kidding!) to 'include this hat in your will'?

What other hat gives you eight water-protected 'brag tags' concealed inside the crown for you to pass on to admiring acquaintances. These brag tags are not just where and how to buy the hat. They include notes, quotes and anecdotes to turn new acquaintances into friends.

Tilley Hats are worth buying. They are well made and faithfully guaranteed. The owners of this company deserve to get rich. Tilley Hats are also worth studying. This product makes the customer rich – information rich.

Key Learning Point

Information *about* a product or service can add tremendous value *to* that product or service.

Action Steps

What useful information can you provide about who you are, what you do, where, why and how? What insights can you collect to teach, tell, instruct, advise, inform, arouse or entertain?

Innovation magnifies your service

Imagine dinner at a romantic restaurant: soft music, candlelight, fine wine. You use a credit card to pay the bill and the waiter brings your receipt.

Can you see those important financial figures on the bottom? Are they large, clear and easy to read? Probably not.

Now what? Do you reach for the magnifying glass you carry routinely in your purse or pocket? Not likely.

Not unless you carry the new 'LensCard' from Chase Manhattan Bank. With a magnifying glass built into the corner of the credit card, this innovation gives Chase customers the magnifying power they need exactly when and where they need it; in the restaurant, at the cash register, whenever those financial little numbers mean a lot.

Key Learning Point

Provide your customers what they need, exactly when and where they need it. Do it before anyone else and you've got a valuable service innovation.

Action Steps

Look carefully. What would make things easier for your customers? How about these: a handy pen or pencil, a hard writing surface, the correct date or time of day, small change for a machine, a calculator, local map, a dictionary, a mobile telephone, telephone directory, soft, absorbent tissues, instant photograph or photocopy facilities, a non-leak plastic bag, notecards, envelope or postage stamps, packing tape, sturdy string, a twist-tie or rubber band, cutting knife, scissors or a screwdriver?

Whatever it is, provide it now. Making things easier for your customers will make business much better for you.

IKEA turns common sense upside down

At IKEA the furniture store, oversized umbrellas sit near the check-out.

The umbrellas are huge (3 people can fit underneath), colorful (in IKEA's signature blue and yellow with a big company logo), and made of good quality materials (strong cloth, steel shaft, large wooden handle). Exactly the kind of umbrella you want to carry when it's raining.

A small sign hangs nearby:

> IKEA UMBRELLAS
> Sunny Day .... $ 10.
> Rainy Day .... $ 3.

I did a double-take, then smiled. Rainy days are when you really *need* an umbrella. Common sense says a smart retailer could raise the price. But IKEA is even smarter.

IKEA wants you to enjoy the convenience of a big umbrella when you need it. They want you to remember the unusually low price. They want you to help promote their stores with a huge IKEA umbrella.

Key Learning Point

IKEA wants you coming back. And with treatment like this, you will.

Action Steps

What 'rainy day' situations hurt *your* customers? Equipment failure? Supplies out of stock? Last-minute delivery needs? Do they expect to pay *more* for urgent, special or last-minute attention? That's the moment to 'turn common sense upside down' and give your customers more than they expect, at less than they expect to pay.

Your income may be lower for a moment, but your revenue will be healthy for a lifetime.

Ireland's 'express lane' makes sense

Remember the last time you were in a supermarket approaching check-out?

Remember the fast-moving line marked 'Express Lane: 6 items or less'?

Have you ever counted the goods inside your basket and then *removed* one or two so you could get into the fast-moving line? I know I have.

What a bizarre concept: rewarding customers with greater speed for purchasing *less* instead of more. This 'common sense' approach is downright counter-productive.

One supermarket in Ireland has turned conventional wisdom on its ear. Their speediest check-out line is clearly marked: 'Express lane: $150 or more.'

This lane is *express!* Extra registers keep the line moving. Big buyers have their purchases rung up simultaneously on two registers by two check-out staff. Extra helpers are on hand at all times to bag the groceries and escort big buyers to their cars. And special coupons are given to encourage repeat business.

With service like this, wouldn't you *add* a few items to your grocery basket to qualify for the Express Lane? Now that's common service sense.

Key Learning Point

Your most valuable customers deserve special service to make their lives easier and their purchases more convenient. That makes sense.

Action Steps

What do *you* do for your big buyers to ensure their repeat business? What special service belongs in *your* organization's Express Lane?

It's not about the price...

Singapore is known world-wide as a leading center for printing attractive books.

But Singapore has a higher cost base (labor, utilities, rent) than many other cities in the region. In a cost-conscious industry like book publishing, how do these apparent contradictions make sense?

I learned the answer first-hand as the first edition of *UP Your Service!* went to press. It's not about the lowest price – it's all about the *service*.

The first edition book cover has a four-color print with embossing, spot varnish and two flaps. The printer's response: 'No problem.'

The interior is 100-gram bright-white wood-free paper with digital photos on every page, thread-sewn for greater durability and value. The printer's response: 'No problem.'

The timeline was excruciatingly tight to get books into the stores in time for a scheduled launch. The printer's response: 'Watch me hustle!' (And hustle he did!)

Speed, quality, logistics, flexibility, hustle. In a city where everything moves quickly, convenience and cooperation run *high*. The ultimate cost to publishers stays *low*.

Key Learning Point

Do you try to win your customers based upon low price? It may not be what they care about most, and not what they'll remember. Often, it's not about the price at all; it's all about the *service*.

Action Steps

Instead of working like mad to give the lowest price, work like crazy to improve the quality of your service. You'll attract customers who value your effort, while earning premium pricing and the profits you rightly deserve.

Million-dollar voice mail

Have you ever heard a voice mail recording so good that you called back twice, just to hear the message? I have.

The Million Dollar Round Table (MDRT) is an international association of top agents in the insurance industry. I called their main office in Chicago after normal business hours. Often that leads a caller to voice mail and many minutes of frustration. Not at the MDRT!

The quality of their voice mail system is so user-friendly, I called back twice just to hear it again.

The welcome message features a friendly voice with terrific tone and clear articulation. The elegance of technical design is obvious as a logical sequence of menus and options is presented. And a dynamite introductory sentence starts the whole thing rolling:

'This is the Million Dollar Round Table. Our lobby is now closed. Regular lobby hours are 8:30 am – 5:00 pm, Central Standard Time. Our 24-hour fax number is 847-518-0696. You now have two options. Option one is…'

What a great idea! Call a voice mail halfway around the world, and find yourself being cared for at 'the Lobby'! A terrific perception point. A magnificent moment of truth.

Key Learning Point

Customers interact with your organization at many different points and places. Each is an opportunity to impress, surprise and delight. No detail should be too small to receive your full and creative attention.

Action Steps

Find a small area where customers interact with your business. Polish it, fine-tune it, improve it until it shines. (One gas station did this by putting fresh flowers in the restroom every day. What will *you* do?)

Palm Pilot wins with positive word-of-mouth

I conducted a program for a large audience in the Philippines. Sponsors included Citibank, Qualcomm and Micro-Warehouse, a distributor of 3Com's Palm Pilot.

We were having a great time raffling away three Palm Pilots, so I asked the audience, 'How many of you actually use a Palm Pilot, and have it with you here today?' Fourteen people responded, and I invited them up on stage.

As they lined up with Palm Pilots in hand, I handed the microphone to the first person and said, 'Please tell us how you feel about your Palm Pilot.' This was totally spontaneous. The first fellow took the microphone and said, 'This is my life!' The second person blurted out, 'I couldn't live without it. All my activities and information are right here!'

The third person, an attractive woman, said, 'This holds *all* my secrets.' The crowd roared. She added, 'Fortunately, it's password protected.' The crowd roared again.

This continued down the line until all fourteen owners had given their short but potent testimonials.

My eye caught the sponsor's face in the back of the room. He was *glowing* with delight. And for good reason: positive word-of-mouth is trusted, remembered and acted upon more than any other form of advertising.

Key Learning Point

Asking for testimonials from your customers makes good sense; sharing these words with others makes good business.

Action Steps

Ask your loyal customers for testimonials for your products and service. Post these affirmative comments where others can read them, enjoy them, and be positively influenced by them.

Little things can mean a lot

At the Westin Chosun Hotel in Seoul, Korea, the rooms are not large, but a few thoughtful touches combine to make a big difference.

There is the usual range of amenities: slippers, bathrobes, room safe, mini-bar, hairdryer, voicemail, etc.

But the bathroom mirror has a heater installed behind it, just above the sink. After a shower when the room is steamy, that small section of mirror remains clear.

There is a box of tissues in the bathroom, of course, but another box sits by the bed in an attractive container.

A laundry bag is waiting when I arrive; that's normal. But inside the closet an empty shopping bag is also provided for my use. It's large and strong and very sleek, silver-colored with dark blue ribbon handles. There is no big brand name of the hotel emblazoned on the side, only an elegant print near the top edge that says: 'Your Bag'.

I think I'll bring it home inside my luggage.

Ever stayed in a hotel room that was big, but not very special? My room at the hotel is just the opposite, small in size but very big in little pleasures.

Key Learning Point

You can use this strategy, too. Make a big impression by paying attention to the little things that count. Maybe it's the personal note you write, or remembering a customer's preference from one visit to another. Perhaps it's pre-filling a form on your customer's behalf, or keeping track of an order and calling ahead to reconfirm delivery.

Action Steps

Your action steps needn't be big, bold or expensive. Often it's the little things that make a big difference in service.

Only 'Top Box Quality' at Motorola

As an organizational goal, 'customer satisfaction' is obsolete. Customers *expect* satisfaction, and many businesses deliver it. Satisfying customers is not enough to ensure you get their praise and future business.

Motorola is one of the original benchmark companies for 'Total Customer Satisfaction' (TCS). Their persistent pursuit of TCS is legendary, with Six Sigma quality programs and 10X campaigns for cycle time reduction.

Motorola now uses a new metric to track 'customer loyalty', and not just 'customer satisfaction'. They ask for a rating of 'Overall Satisfaction', and ask if the customer intends to *purchase again* from Motorola. And they ask if the customer will willingly *recommend* Motorola to others.

Motorola's target is genuine *customer loyalty*, which includes high satisfaction, a commitment to future business, and sharing positive word-of-mouth. Motorola won't be satisfied until customers check the 'top box' in all three areas.

Key Learning Point

Customer satisfaction only measures customer opinion for a fleeting moment in time. But good customer relationships are not fleeting. They are continuous. They have history, and present moments, and rich, fulfilling futures.

Action Steps

How can you apply these lessons? When you survey customers, don't just ask 'Are you not satisfied, somewhat satisfied, very satisfied.' Take the initiative to find out whether your customer is planning to buy from you again in the future. If so, how soon? If not, why not? Then ask if your customer will 'refer you enthusiastically to others'? If so, why are they enthusiastic? If not, what needs to change for *customers* to become *advocates* for your products and your service?

10

BUILDING UP YOUR BUSINESS

'Reach the heights of superior service by
building your business each day.'

1:1 – The next wave in customer care

What's next after customer satisfaction?

In their bestselling book, *The One to One Future*, Martha Rogers and Don Peppers offer some useful answers.

To keep customers coming back, Peppers and Rogers highlight four key approaches:

1. *Recognize your most valuable customers.* Provide special deals, unique acknowledgments, prestige club status, surprise gifts, etc.

2. *Create loyalty award programs.* Buy ten – get one free, frequent flyer miles, bonus awards for repeat business, etc.

3. *Provide outstanding customer satisfaction.* Doing a top quality job is still key. Deliver what you promise, when you promise, and more.

4. *Build learning relationships.* Collaborate with customers to tailor your service delivery 'just the way they want it'. Over time, your company will deliver service that is so customized, your customers won't bother to teach other companies how to serve them as well.

For example, imagine an airline that keeps track of your telephone number, meal, drink and seat preference, whether or not you like to be left alone during long flights, your favorite choice of reading materials, and your personal sports or hobbies. Then imagine they actually integrate this information with their reservations office, check-in desk and cabin crew. Now imagine the staff are trained to refer graciously to this information while serving you.

I've had several airlines ask me to complete their 'premier passenger' questionnaires, but none seem to actually *use* the information I provide. If one airline staff member (on the phone, at the check-in counter or in the air) would simply say, 'Welcome back, Mr. Kaufman. Have you had any good scuba-dives lately?', my eyes would go wide with surprise, and my sense of loyalty and connection with that airline would certainly jump!

Key Learning Point

Don't settle for mere 'customer satisfaction'. Build loyal, long-lasting relationships. Know who are your most valuable customers. Understand how and why they use your services or products. Remember their preferences and adapt your delivery to give them what they want, when they want it, the way they want it.

Action Steps

There are many steps you can take to move your company in this direction. Start by signing up for Peppers and Rogers free e-mail newsletter. It's one of the most interesting pieces of e-mail I receive each week. You can subscribe by visiting their website at www.1to1.com

Credibility comes from the customer

At a recent tourism industry conference, the participants explored how effective partnerships could help boost travel to their region.

A long chain of 'travel partners' was involved, including national tourism boards, wholesalers, travel agents, airlines, hotels, taxis and transport companies, restaurants, tourist attractions, shopping malls, medical facilities, media representatives and even banks.

The panel discussion was lively. The airline suggested the media should lower advertising rates. The journalist said national tourism boards should provide more up-to-date information. Restaurants asked travel agents to pre-book special meals. Transport companies wanted to tie-in with tourist attractions to ensure all-day bookings.

And everyone wanted the media to run only glowing reports and attractive photographs to lure the tourists closer.

These industry professionals were so busy pointing to the others in the room, they missed the most important 'travel partner' of them all – a truly delighted tourist.

After all, which is more likely to influence your choice of a vacation destination? A colorful magazine advertisement? Or a colorful story from your next-door neighbor about his fantastic holiday in the land of his dreams?

Which do you find more credible? A commercial with actresses promising 'smiles in the air', or a candid comment from your colleague about the incredible service she receives aboard her favorite airline?

I wonder why the travel industry doesn't put more emphasis on cultivating *positive word-of-mouth* from delighted customers as the most important and effective 'promotional partners'?

For example, premium travelers often receive a basket of

fruit and a signed 'Welcome' message from the hotel General Manager upon arrival. That's so common it's become expected.

How would the same traveler feel if he received a personal 'Thank You' note from the General Manager after returning home? Now that might make a difference!

How many airlines routinely say 'Thank you for flying with us' over the public announcement system, but never make personal eye-contact while wishing you a truly good day?

Most taxi drivers remember where you are going, but forget how to say 'Thank you' when you get there.

Every restaurant gives you a menu to read and a bill at the end of the meal, but how many give you a small coupon or voucher as you leave to invite you back?

Every tourist attraction and shopping mall has restrooms for your convenience, but how many are kept shining clean?

Key Learning Point

Industry partners should cooperate to build a better future. But remember, the greatest partner for your prosperity, progress and promotion is a truly delighted customer.

Action Steps

The next time you attend an industry conference, notice how much time and attention is paid to companies, politics and well-known industry players. Be sure the majority of *your* time is invested where it gives you the highest return: in attracting, delighting and keeping your best clients.

How much service is *too much* service?

People often ask, 'What level of service should we strive to provide? Should we give "Unbelievable!" service if our customers are not willing to pay for it?'

My answer is definitely *no!*

Don't go to the moon on service if your business model on the moon doesn't work. No sense 'serving yourself to death', bending over backwards but going broke in the process.

You need to determine what level of service your business can provide, and match that with what your customers are willing to pay.

Take note: customers rarely put voluntary limits on their service expectations. That's why making *clear service agreements* is so important to you...and your customers.

You must communicate clearly what you promise to provide, and what you are *not* promising, too!

The manager of a local Internet Service Provider (ISP) approached me with this relevant complaint:

His staff go into customers' homes and offices to install modems and communications software. They train their customers to access new e-mail accounts and surf the World Wide Web.

Before his staff can leave, however, office-based customers start asking about unrelated hardware compatibility, new software upgrades and suggestions on how to fix non-working printers!

Eager home-based customers insist on help installing new games and joysticks, debugging new versions of Windows, even assistance repairing their children's Nintendo!

His staff's explanation that, 'We are just an Internet Service Provider, not a computer repair service', seem to fall upon deaf ears. As far as his customers are concerned,

'You are the computer people, and we have a computer problem. Now that you are in our home or office...fix it!'

One look at his brochure reveals the source of the problem. It reads: 'Enter the digital age! Modernize your life! Capture the computer advantage!'

Plenty of glittering encouragements to buy, but no clear and detailed listing of the *actual service promise*.

To eliminate the problem, this company must clarify and specify what services they do provide...and what services they do not.

For example:

We provide A, B and C.

We do not provide X, Y or Z in the normal service package.

We can arrange X, Y and Z for you at an additional charge, or

We have associates who can do X, Y and Z. Reliable referrals are provided on request.

Key Learning Point

Be sure the service agreements you make with your customers and internal partners are complete and clear. Misunderstanding can lead to disappointment once delivery of your service is underway.

Action Steps

Check with your customers and staff. Find out where misunderstanding and disagreements arise. Then look closely at your proposals, contracts and service level agreements. Wherever uncertainty is found, replace it with accuracy, clarity and understanding.

Note: Don't use this principle to avoid regularly *upgrading* your service agreements. With technology you may improve the quality of your service *without* increasing your costs. (Your competitors are working on it now.)

Customer satisfaction is a rearview mirror

What is the difference between customer satisfaction and customer loyalty?

One package delivery company uses a regular survey to measure customer satisfaction: shipping volume (increasing, decreasing or stable), error rate (packages lost, damaged or delayed), and customer rating (happy, neutral or upset).

While these indicators provide a valid snapshot of performance and customer opinion, they are lagging rather than leading, like looking in the rearview mirror.

The difference between customer satisfaction and customer loyalty is illustrated by these future-facing indicators now being used by the delivery company:

1. *Future business:* How strong is your customer's intention and commitment to do business with you in the future? (Absolutely – Maybe – Definitely not)

2. *Positive word-of-mouth:* How vigorously do customers praise and recommend you to others? (Enthusiastic referrals – Make no effort – Tell others to stay away)

3. *Constructive feedback:* Do your customers help you upgrade your service and improve your organization? (Give you lots of ideas and inputs – Keep quiet, even when things go wrong – Tells the competition about your weakness)

Key Learning Point

Measuring customer satisfaction is important, but the future lies before you, not behind.

Action Steps

Measure your customer's loyalty, not just their current satisfaction. Use leading questions to fathom their intentions about the future.

Twenty words to build a better future

If you want to increase sales, enhance customer service or consistently improve performance, ask your customers this question (20 words):

'Is there anything we could do differently the next time that would make it better or more valuable for you?'

This simple question tells customers you are looking to the future, seeking to improve, and grateful for their feedback.

If you want to work more productively between departments, or more effectively with the members of your team, memorize and utilize this question (20 words):

'Is there anything we could do differently the next time that would make it better or more valuable for you?'

Colleagues will understand you are receptive, not defensive. You welcome new possibilities, approaches and ideas.

If you want a better home or family life, sincerely ask your loved ones this very simple question (20 words):

'Is there anything I could do differently the next time that would make it better or more valuable for you?' (I changed one word in the sentence. Find it?)

Key Learning Point

When you close a sale, finish a job or complete a project, don't just wait around for 'the next time'. Initiate the conversation for improvement. Your discussion will lead to better relationships, understanding and results.

Action Steps

Repeat this sentence until you can do it from memory, then use it consistently with your customers, colleagues and partners (20 words):

'Is there anything we could do differently the next time that would make it better or more valuable for you?'

The customer's tastebuds are always right

When I tasted the Greenwich Pizza 'Garden Delight' in the Philippines, my tastebuds got a shock!

The pizza was covered with *sweet* tomato sauce and the cheese on top was *cheddar*.

I've been eating pizza all my life. Pizza is made with tangy tomato sauce and should be covered with mozzarella cheese, right? Sweet sauce and cheddar is no way to make a pizza.

Unless you want to sell a *lot* of pizza in the Philippines.

Greenwich Pizza doesn't *care* what pizza is known for in Italy or New York or anywhere else for that matter. Greenwich wants to dominate the Philippine pizza market. As far as they're concerned, when you are in the Philippines, Philippine tastebuds rule.

If the local market wants sweet, then sweet tomato sauce it is. If local customers prefer cheddar, spread on the cheddar cheese.

Global brands Pizza Hut, Shakeys and Dominos all sell pizza in the Philippines. But local Greenwich is the market leader.

Why? Because Pizza Hut, Shakeys and Dominos all make their pizza to global (not local) pizza standards. With plenty of tangy tomato sauce and mozzarella cheese.

Key Learning Point

Question: Who knows best what customers really want? Local businesses or global corporations?

Answer: Neither. The people who know best what customers really want are the customers themselves!

Action Steps

Do you think you already know what's best for your customers? Or do you really *listen* to learn what your customers prefer?

The positive power of competition

I left my mobile telephone in a taxi and went sheepishly to buy a replacement. The people at the telephone company were patient as I selected a new mobile phone.

One week later I realized I had chosen a new model a bit too big for my liking. I tried to sell my (almost new) phone at a steep discount to someone else, but found no one eager to buy.

I called the telephone company to ask where people go to sell their mobile phones. The staff quickly offered to take back the (almost new) telephone and replace it with another model. I was amazed.

I was even more amazed by the service at the counter. The staff took back my (almost new) phone, batteries, charger and carrying case at full price value. They worked with me patiently for 40 minutes evaluating other phones of smaller size. Then they calculated that they still owed me $14 in the exchange. (I bought an extra battery to even things up.)

The phone company wasn't always this way.

Then I recalled the recent arrival of a feisty competitor on the scene. To stay in business, the telephone company must keep customers happy. That means doing things differently and better than before.

Key Learning Point

Vigorous competition may be the best thing that ever happened to customer service. It wakes people up and makes them serve you better.

Action Steps

Welcome your competitors. They challenge you to upgrade and improve your service. This helps you stay alert, and keeps your customers happy.

Add value first, *reap* value later

 I was teaching about customer intimacy and loyalty when one participant asked, 'What if your competitor has already built a close relationship with a customer, and you want to get inside?'

I replied, '*Add* value first. You will *reap* value later.'

How can you help prospective customers right now – even before they become your paying customers?

Can you send articles of interest with your namecard attached? Could you make practical suggestions to help them serve *their* customers better? Can you provide insight about developments in your industry that may soon impact theirs? Could you write notes of congratulations when they succeed in a major project or undertaking?

If you add value high enough or long enough, eventually you will get a piece of your prospect's business. It may not be a big piece, but it will be a start. Do a fabulous job delivering that first piece of business and more work will surely follow.

Key Learning Point

This principle applies in business – and in life. When you give enough, long enough, eventually *you will receive.*

Action Steps

Make a contribution to those who are not yet your customers, but whom you would like to have as customers one day. Deliver with quality and consistency that surprises in a positive way. One day these prospects will become valuable customers – yours.

I do this every month with the free newsletter, *The Best of Active Learning.* Get your free subscription at www.RonKaufman.com

Give a gift that gives again

Many companies encourage customer loyalty with discounts and other gifts. These may be appreciated, but it can also become expensive and expected.

Here's another idea that will make your customers happy and also boost your business.

Send your existing customers a free coupon for some of your products or your service. But make this voucher valid *only* when signed by your current customer, and redeemable *only* by someone who is not (yet) your customer.

What does this accomplish?

Your existing customer gets a valuable gift to share with someone else. Your new customer gets a gift from someone they respect, and a valuable introduction to you. You do something nice for existing customers, get a brand new customer, and find out which of your current customers will help your business grow.

This simple approach spreads good value and goodwill for everyone.

Key Learning Point

Giving a 'free gift' to your existing customers may be appreciated, but may also become expected. Giving them a free gift to share with someone else can be a unique surprise for both.

Action Steps

Decide which of your current customers are most valuable to you. It is likely they know others like themselves. Decide what you are willing to give away as an introductory free gift. Then match your customer list with your intended free gift in the 'pass it on' manner outlined above. Watch your existing customers smile and your new customers arrive, to the surprise and benefit of all.

Beta means never having to say you're sorry

I recently heard a technology presentation from a young but experienced CEO of a big 'clicks and mortar' organization. He told the large audience confidently, 'Beta means never having to say you're sorry.'

'That's right,' I thought to myself. 'When launching the beta test of a new web-enabled process, customers must understand it's only a pilot run and should be forgiving if things mess up or don't work out as planned.'

I was totally wrong about his point of view.

In direct contrast to my thinking, this e-commerce veteran explained that new web-based interactions often do *not* work properly during a beta test.

However, *from the customer's point of view*, he insisted, your pilot run must be successful enough to avoid creating negative customer perceptions or the need to apologize after the fact.

The cost and consequences of doing it badly are customer skepticism, hesitation and negative word-of-mouth. That's a cost too high to pay in today's fast-moving world of instant communications.

Key Learning Point

If you are planning the design and launch of a new customer interface or web-enabled process, be sure to have enough staff and resources on hand to execute brilliantly *from the customer's point of view*, even if the technology itself proves problematic.

Action Steps

Plan ahead, staff up and allocate more resources than you will require. When you do launch, do whatever it takes to create a positive customer experience. Keep your breakdowns and learning behind the scenes. Make sure your customer is well satisfied and well served out in front.

Give yourself a vigorous visual audit

I recently visited my university alma mater in the United States.

This Ivy League institution is a powerhouse of education and research. But you wouldn't know it from the huge cracks and peeling paint on the walls of the Student Union.

The Student Union is not where traditional academic work is done; it's not a library or a lab.

But the Student Union *is* where students sip coffee and read the paper. It's where prospective students and their parents 'take in the atmosphere' and assess the student body. And it's where alumni go to feel proud of their college days and reconnect with the campus.

Millions are spent annually on research facilities and excellent faculty members, but not enough money is spent on simple maintenance to keep the Student Union looking sharp.

I was embarrassed by the dilapidation and left the campus disappointed.

Key Learning Point

Give yourself a vigorous visual audit. Your customers do it every day.

Action Steps

What can you do now to improve your visual image? How about: change the toner cartridge in your printer, cut away dead leaves on your office plants, update or remove old items hanging on the walls, find a better place to stash that box gathering dust in the corner, create an e-mail signature that projects a positive image, get a haircut, shine your shoes, throw out whatever is no longer current, replace every light bulb that isn't working, scrub down the walks and the handrails, put on a fresh coat of paint. Take a look around you. I am sure you can see many more.

Give yourself an auditory audit

I was in Santa Fe, New Mexico and got a wake-up call in my hotel room. I had asked for 6:30 am. The call came at 6:43.

I had an early morning appointment, so the delay was indeed unwelcome. But the automated wake-up message was worse. It said, 'Good morning. This is your wake-up call. The time is 7:30 am.'

The automated hotel wake-up system had gone off the correct time by an hour and thirteen minutes.

I wondered how long it had been that way. I wondered how many other guests had heard equally off-base recordings. I wondered if the hotel management or staff would ever discover the problem.

Being the kind of guy I am, I called the Front Office to tell them about the situation. A disinterested morning voice replied, 'Thank you. I'll tell someone to do something about it.' I wondered if she would.

Later in the week I stayed at the JFK Hilton in New York. I asked for a wake-up call at 6:00 am. The call came at 6:00 am sharp, but the crude recording had all the vocal appeal of a mugging in process: 'This is a wake-up call from the Hilton at JFK.' Click. Buzz. Over.

In Singapore, I often call upon a local association that employs the handicapped for office projects. They do a great job with assembly, mailing and database input. But their telephone system is a nightmare.

If you get transferred from one caller to another, or get put 'on hold' during the conversation, you will *hear* the pain. Loud static. Loud radio station static. The kind of static you get when the radio is not tuned to any particular station, but the volume is cranked up high!

I've told them about it five times, but they haven't fixed

the problem. After all, they don't hear it. They don't put themselves on hold.

Key Learning Point

Listen up! You can learn from these misadventures. Auditory perception points make a big difference to your customers and colleagues.

Action Steps

Double-check your voice mail message. Listen to your on-hold words and music. Write warm and welcoming scripts for all your telephone staff. Pay attention to the musical background in your office and lobby areas. And put a smile on your face. We can hear it in the sound of your voice.

Customer loyalty – in the hospital?

Does seeking 'customer loyalty' make any sense in a hospital setting?

Most people try to *avoid* becoming patients. But bodies do need medical care from time to time.

Providing that care to repeat customers can be profitable for doctors, hospitals and medical centers. But it might be awkward for your doctor to say, 'I look forward to seeing you again soon.'

To build a successful practice, every doctor should give a high level of technical care (diagnosis and treatment) coupled with an equally high level of personal care (assurance, education and compassion).

Technical care is essential – no one wants an incompetent doctor. But personal care can make all the difference between one medical service provider and another.

I visited two dentists for treatment of a troublesome tooth.

Dentist A was highly recommended, but the office was spartan and the ambience cold and tense. I quickly forgot his name.

Dr. Peter Tay was also well recommended, but his office was quite a surprise.

I found pleasant surroundings, a vast array of magazines, plenty of educational literature, attractive posters and paintings on the wall. Inspirational music played in the lobby. A range of other music was available for my personal listening pleasure. There was even a pantry with hot and cold drinks and a refrigerator with healthy snacks for light refreshment.

The nurses were genuinely cheerful. The telephone receptionist almost chirped!

And the dentist? Clearly, he *enjoys* working in this office.

When my treatment was finally done, Dr. Tay smiled and said, 'I shouldn't say we look forward to seeing you again soon, but if you ever need our care in the future, you know where to find us.'

He's right. I'm *not* keen to go back for similar treatment. But I do get regular check-ups, and every six-month cleanings. And I make many enthusiastic referrals.

All that repeat business goes to the same dentist. Dentist A or Dr. Peter Tay? You can guess which one.

Key Learning Point

If you want customers coming back again and again to *your* business, be competent at what you do – that's essential. But also take the time to be assuring, informative, comforting and kind.

Even in medical situations (emergencies aside) people have a choice about where to go, and who to recommend.

Action Steps

Do all you can to be the best you can in your chosen profession. Improve your skills, raise your standards, upgrade your certification. But also improve your surroundings, your office and the environment in which you work.

Your skills and space go hand in hand in the eyes, ears and hearts of your customers.

What is Ron's website really for?

I decided to upgrade my website and contacted four developers to get opinions and quotations. What an unsettling experience!

The first developer spoke at length about the need to set up 'links, links, links!' to every other service quality, professional speaking, teambuilding and corporate training site on the Net. He was convinced that 'no site is an island' and offered to 'link, link, link!' and then send out 'spam, spam, spam!' in order to get more traffic to the site.

An interesting point of view, although I am not sure about all that 'spamming'. I moved to the second developer.

'Your site has got to be *sticky*!', she enthused. 'It's not enough to get visitors to come. You've got to keep them coming *back*! Get your visitors to complete a questionnaire explaining who they are, what they do, where they live and what's really important in their lives,' she explained. 'Then build a restricted area for members only. And issue each member a special password allowing them restricted access to limited domains.'

Restricted areas are not quite my style...and this highly individualized approach would certainly add a layer of complexity. Still, the range of ideas she offered was indeed intriguing.

On to developer number three where the name of their game is 'e-commerce'. An intensive tutorial updated me to the possibilities (and complexities) of e-commerce. Secure servers. Encryption. Online credit card processing. Integrated inventory and shipping functions. EDI with real-time links the banks.

You can buy many video-based learning systems at the Ron Kaufman website, so the need for e-commerce solutions is real. But how enhanced should that solution be? And how soon? And, by the way, how much does it cost? Hmmm...good questions.

The fourth developer was the most graphically oriented, promoting animations and 'shocked' presentations: moving images, spinning objects and very little text. They were clear in their minds that my entire site needed a visual over-haul of substantial proportion.

I explained that *all* Ron Kaufman presentation materials share the same visual identity. Brochures, workbooks, video programs and even the website have a common graphic 'look'...carefully created and developed over the years.

'So if you Internet folks make a dramatic change to the look of the entire website,' I started...'Exactly,' they jumped in with excitement, 'then all the other materials will have to be changed, too!' Not quite what I had in mind.

Each of the developers were deeply enamored of their own expertise. Each was eager to 'sell' me on the importance (nay, necessity!) of implementing *their* solutions. Though several queried me later for a list of my specifications, none *began* the conversation with a keen intent to explore what I wanted to *achieve* at the website.

Key Learning Point

Sometimes we become so expert in our own professions we forget that clients may be less familiar with the domain. Think about being a patient in a hospital. Don't you appreciate the effort to educate you and set you at ease as much as the medicine provided? What about a visit to the car mechanic or the accountant? Isn't having a background of trust and confidence as important as having the right work done?

Action Steps

Invest the time and effort, upfront, to build your rapport with prospects and customers on *their* terms. Don't just leap in with your bold (and possibly brilliant) recommendations. Explore thoroughly first. Suggest solutions later.

WHEN THINGS GO WRONG

'When things don't come out the way you expected,
you expect things should get worked out!'

Don't be a softie...*squeak*!

I advocate living in an appreciative manner. It spreads goodwill and attracts good service.

But wait! I'm not suggesting you simply float in a cloud of good feelings hoping that everyone serves you well.

Sometimes you get *bad* service. And when that happens to you, *squeak*! Why? Because the old saying is true: the squeaky wheel gets the grease.

When you need more attention, better help, stronger support or valid compensation, here's what you can do:

1. *Get your facts straight.* Put them down in writing, avoiding the temptation to inflate or exaggerate your claims.

2. *Speak or write to someone who can help.* Over the phone, be sure you talk with someone who can make things happen (sometimes a secretary can get things done more quickly than a manager). When writing, send your letter to a 'real person', not to a faceless 'Office of Customer Affairs'.

3. *Explain your situation.* Detail the problem, specify your request (be reasonable here), and give a timeline for receiving a reply (10–14 days is fair in most situations).

4. *Escalate your communication.* If you do *not* get a response by the given date explain that you will promptly complain to the President, General Manager or Managing Director. Don't make it sound like a threat, but let them know you are ready to do what's necessary to get the satisfaction you require.

5. *Take even stronger action.* Loyal customers are important to every business, so your chances of being well attended are getting better all the time. However, in the unlikely event you do *not* get the satisfaction you deserve, then take stronger action.

Write to your local newspaper, contact the Better Business Bureau, send out a message to your friends and colleagues, tell the competition, or even get more 'creative' with the nature and the style of your complaint.

I've seen customers create and pay for negative newspaper ads, websites, pickets, boycotts and PowerPoint presentations that spread like a virus.

While I am not advocating antagonism for its own sake, when you need attention and it's not forthcoming, you gotta do what you gotta do.

Key Learning Point

When you want a response, reaction or rapid resolution to a service problem, be sure your voice is heard. Remember, complaining about lousy service helps businesses to improve. If they don't pay attention to what's going wrong, they'll just keep doing it to others.

Action Steps

Follow the five steps listed the next time *you* have a service problem. And keep track of the details: your complaint, their response and the ultimate resolution. If they do a *good* job, be sure to let them know. Stop squeaking, and start speaking, with praise.

How to put loyalty at risk

I am a loyal customer. My suppliers help me build my business and enjoy my busy life. I recommend them enthusiastically to others, buy from them repeatedly and rarely challenge them on price. But there comes a point...

Every month I ship packages to customers around the world. My courier company had a 'bonus program' to encourage and reward customer loyalty. Two years ago the program offered a cash discount for volume shipping. Last year the program was changed to provide shopping and dining vouchers instead of discounts. A new approach – fair enough.

At the end of the year I was clearing out files and realized I had never received a single dining or shopping voucher. I contacted the courier company and was told, 'Since you already get a special corporate rate, you are no longer eligible for the bonus.'

That was odd. The company never mentioned this when they first changed the terms of the program. In fact, they had sent me a detailed letter describing the new program benefits, and promised to send me a monthly statement.

Then the representative said, 'But if you like, your shipping volume is high enough to that we can increase your corporate discount rate from 26% to 40%.'

That was odd, too. My shipping volume has been fairly consistent for several years. Now very curious, I asked, 'When did I qualify for a 40% discount rate?'

The representative studied my account and replied, 'About two years ago.'

That was more than odd; that was upsetting. For two years I had qualified for a lower shipping rate, but the courier company never told me. Then they disqualified me from their new bonus program, and never informed me.

I said to the representative: 'My loyalty to your company is at risk. You folks need to do some recovery, and fast.'

The representative's response has been gradual and measured. There has been no surge of beneficial activity, no act of generosity or special gesture, no personalized effort to reclaim lost goodwill. I asked twice in writing for the name and e-mail address of the General Manager. My requests have been ignored.

If you were me, what would your reaction be? Here's mine: I opened a new account with their competition.

Key Learning Point

Your loyal customers deserve your best available deals and discounts. Don't ever take them for granted. You may think you can charge them more for a while, and only change later 'if they find out'. But there's a problem with that approach: when they do find out, they may not want to be your customer any more.

Furthermore, if something happens and your loyal customer feels burned, abused or taken for granted, you'd better *hustle* to set things right! Just 'fixing the problem' won't be enough. You need to take fast action and great care of the person who feels the problem.

Action Steps

Do a rigorous review of your special pricing, packages and promotions. Make sure you offer your best customers the best you have to offer.

Review your service recovery plans, policies and implementation. Loyal customers are worth retaining. Short-term costs, effort or embarrassment are a small price to pay for long-term purchases, profits and support.

Who were they designing it for?

I am regularly amazed by brand new facilities that are obviously user-unfriendly. Huge investments of time and money...but who are they designing it for?!

A new airport in the Middle East is an impressive and expensive building. It's huge, packed with stainless steel and halogen lights and lots of fancy gold.

But it takes six escalators, two moving sidewalks and 3,446 steps (I counted) to get from the aircraft door to the taxi door at curbside. And no baggage trolleys are provided.

What were the architects thinking about? Size? Grandeur? Physical exercise? Who were they designing it for?!

A sparkling new hotel opened in a major capital city. There is no clear signage directing guests from the ballrooms to the restrooms. The few signs that do exist are etched in muted gold on dark marble pillars.

More obvious signage was considered inappropriate for such elegant decor. Very stylish, very chic. But who were they designing it for?!

I received a business card with a realtor's mailing address printed in four-point type. That's *very* tiny print (less than half the size of these letters!) Graphic designers love tiny type. It's so trendy, hip and cool. But it's certainly not easy to read.

Who – and – what is a business card for?

I had to argue with the graphics company to print all the contact information in 14 point type on my stationery. (That's bigger than these letters.) They said it was 'too big, not nice, not sophisticated'. I said it had to be big to remain legible, even as 'a fax of a fax'.

Try it with *your* stationery right now.

Fax a copy of your stationery to a friend, and ask her to fax it back to you. Now you have 'a fax of a fax'. It happens a lot in business.

Now look closely at your contact information. If you have a 5, 6, 8 or 9 in your telephone number, is that number still easy to read? If the letter 'i' or 'l' appears in your mailing address, is it easy to distinguish those letters?

Who designed your stationery? Who approved your stationery? Who is your stationery really for?

At a new airline lounge in Hong Kong, a partition of colorful glass hangs from the ceiling. My luggage lightly brushed against it as I walked inside. The entire partition shook and several panels came undone.

A staff member hurried over and began carefully reassembling the panels. (Thank goodness nothing broke.) I felt was embarrassed and apologized profusely.

'Don't worry,' she replied calmly. 'This happens all the time.'

An airport lounge is a heavy traffic area. People are always moving in and out. What were the interior designers thinking? Who were they designing it for?!

Key Learning Point

It's easy to get caught up in designing new things that are 'cool' or 'elegant' or 'hot'. But if you don't keep your customer in mind throughout, you could end up with an investment that's 'not'.

Action Steps

Review your physical surroundings, points of customer interaction, your product, packaging and procedures.

Find something that could be clearer, more helpful or more 'customer-friendly'. And once you find it, fix it.

Why is this information hidden?

Sue forwarded me a strange e-mail she received from a catalog retailer in the United Kingdom.

The message says: 'We can confirm your order details;

Estimated delivery date: 16.10.2001
Order reference number: BA01
Total order value: 68.37

Unfortunately, Item 107-694 is currently unavailable. We have a substitute which is a similar item but all cream in colour. If you would like the substitute item sent please contact us by telephone or by e-mail.

Best Regards, Online Customer Care

What in the world is 'Item 107-694'? How strange that the company tells her the item code and available colors, but does not mention a name or description of the product.

The company asks Sue to contact them either by telephone or by e-mail, but no telephone number is provided.

Such simple information. So obvious to the company. Why is it hidden from the customer?

Key Learning Point

Don't expect customers to know or remember everything about your products and organization. Customers appreciate convenient references and reminders. Make it *easy* for customers to contact, query, try and buy.

Action Steps

Put complete access information on all your products, packages and points of contact. List your mailing and e-mail address, telephone and fax numbers on every page of your website. Put stickers with the same information on the back, bottom or side of all your products. Be sure the signature file in your e-mail program is accurate, detailed and up to date. Make it *easy* for customers to find you, know you and love you.

Who put sand in the grease?

The world is racing towards seamless commerce and instant communications. Fast computers and networks provide the grease.

But *people* design the business processes we use. And sometimes, someone puts sand in the grease.

A local college ordered two copies of my video-based learning programs. They had my pricelist and knew exactly what they wanted. I was the only supplier.

But their Finance Department insisted upon sending a 'request for quotation', then receiving a 'written proposal' so they could send a 'purchase order' from which I would provide an 'approved invoice' – all before delivering the products! That's a lot of paper back and forth (hardcopies required, in duplicate) without a smidgen of added value.

One government agency ordered the entire Ron Kaufman learning library. The products were delivered promptly with our usual invoice enclosed.

But the agency insisted our invoice be re-written as it was dated February 28, the same day as shipment, while the products were delivered on March 1.

Finance refused to accept our invoice as it was dated before delivery, even though the invoice accompanied the products and the products were now delivered.

Key Learning Point

The need for speed in today's economy is real. Get rid of the sand that grinds the gears and slows everything down. Grease up!

Action Steps

Look closely at your business processes and procedures. What can be streamlined? What can be reduced? What can be eliminated altogether?

How to *lose* a customer for life

My friend Benny told me about a local restaurant that serves a variety of Chinese *dim sum* dishes. He went there with five friends for a business lunch and ordered widely from the menu. Each dish featured six bite-sized items, one per person.

Most of the food was delicious, but one tofu dish did not measure up. All six diners popped the tofu into their mouths. Then all six turned up their noses at the taste. The tofu had gone rancid.

Tofu disintegrates pretty quickly in the mouth, so everyone swallowed hard and reached quickly for their drinks to wash away the taste. The waitress apologized right away and promised to tell the owner. Better-tasting dishes soon followed.

But when the bill was presented at the end of the meal, the tofu dish was still included! The waitress apologized again and referred to the restaurant owner. The owner appeared and defended the bill. 'But you ate the tofu,' he said, 'so we still have to charge you. If the tofu was no good, why did you eat all six pieces?' Despite their protests, the tofu remained on the bill.

And that was the last bill ever paid at that restaurant by any of the six lunchtime diners...or their families...or their friends...or their business associates.

Now, what *should* the owner have done? Provide free desserts or a round of free drinks for everyone at the table? Immediately remove the tofu from the bill? Apologize personally and thank the group for their valuable feedback? Promise to alert the chef immediately, and do so? Upon departure, give each of the six diners a business card from the restaurant with a hand-signed promise from the owner for 'Six delicious and fresh tofu *dim sum*...free anytime within the next two months'? All of the above?

This approach would help ensure that each diner returned

in the near future, giving the restaurant – and the tofu – another chance. But no one eats just tofu. So there would be another round of lunchtime bills to pay by each diner...and their families...and their friends...and their business associates.

Key Learning Point

Occasionally things do go sour. When it happens to you, fix the problem *fast*. Make it your speed, generosity and concern that gets remembered. Not the trouble, or the tofu.

Action Steps

Develop a service recovery policy and display it with pride. Let your customers know: if something goes wrong, you will make it right.

An upgrade is usually worse, at first

I recently upgraded the telephone system in our home and office. For the next two days everything about the phones went wrong: crossed lines, disconnected calls, non-working outlets, strange buzzing sounds.

Only after two additional visits by the technician was the upgrade working as intended.

Have you noticed how often this happens?

The new improved computer software runs slower than the version you just replaced. The latest hardware proves harder to manage than the system you abandoned. The new car goes back to the shop for an adjustment within two weeks when the old car worked perfectly for years. The new home has a door that jams, a roof that leaks, a window or floorboard that squeaks.

No one intends an 'upgrade' to start out as a 'downgrade', but the pattern is familiar and occurs frequently.

Key Learning Point

Be upfront with your customers about glitches or hiccups that may occur – and be ready to provide help and reassurance through the early stages of implementation.

Action Steps

If you are upgrading or changing your service in ways that affect your customers, send them advance warning and acknowledge openly what everyone already knows: things go wrong, upgrades take time, it takes effort to locate and iron out the wrinkles.

Be positive and proactive about problems that may occur. Use honesty to build a bond of truth and a commitment to constructive collaboration.

And, if you are the customer, be prepared to hurdle the hiccups!

12

SERVICE RECOVERY = CUSTOMER LOYALTY

'When things go wrong, you have a great opportunity to set them right. Make the most of it!'

It was an accident! (Now what do you do?)

Imagine you are the manager of a fast-food service restaurant.

A mother comes in for lunch with her young son. Half way through the meal the child knocks his drink on the floor creating a *big mess*!

What's the first thing your well-trained crew members should do? Clean the floor? Replace the drink?

Not if you care about your customers and your reputation for quality service.

First, take care of the mother. For her there's personal upset, social embarrassment, a disappointed child and good money spilled on the floor. With a genuine smile you say, 'Don't worry. This happens all the time.'

Let her know the spill will be cleaned up quickly and a replacement drink brought over right away.

Second, put the child at ease. In his mind there may be loss or sadness about the drink, and concern (even fear) about his mother's reaction. With a cheery face, you say brightly, 'Well, accidents do happen!'

Tell him to watch carefully as your 'service professionals' clean up the spill. 'And by the way, a brand new drink for you is already on the way.'

Third, clean up the mess. Your service professionals should do the work with speed and obvious pride.

Fourth, replace the drink. But bring a new drink one size *larger* than the original order. Or, if the spilled drink was already a 'large', then bring along a side-order of french fries or a nice piece of pie.

Give them something extra, something unexpected, something that will be joyfully remembered long after the spill is forgotten.

'But wait!', you wonder. 'Won't everyone start spilling drinks if one person gets this extra generous service?'

In a single word, *no*.

If other customers have been watching from the beginning (and everyone does when a drink hits the floor), they'll be as relieved as the mother and child.

The only thing to increase will be your reputation for superior service, not the number of spilled drinks!

Key Learning Point

When things go wrong, take good care of the people first, the technical issues after. Your procedures should turn your upset customers into enthusiastic advocates. When your customers win, you win.

Action Steps

Check your service recovery procedures. Make sure the first thing on the list is making a positive personal connection through competent customer care.

Total recovery = customer delight

Douglas, an elected delegate at the Democratic National Convention in the United States, dropped his Handspring Visor personal digital assistant (PDA) onto the stone floor of his downtown hotel lobby.

The outer case of the PDA was chipped in one corner, but the software and the system still worked. He called Handspring to purchase a replacement cover.

'Nothing doing,' Handspring customer service replied. They insisted that he needed a completely new Visor.

'No way!', Douglas retorted. 'Why should I buy a new Visor, costing hundreds of dollars, just to replace a plastic part worth a dollar or two at most?'

'Oh no,' the representative assured him. 'The new Visor won't cost you a penny. Your current Visor is still under warranty.'

The representative promised to ship a brand new Visor to him immediately, and then explained that Douglas could ship the old unit back in the very same box. She apologized that the deadline had passed for next day delivery, so the new PDA would arrive in two days instead.

Two days later, as promised, a small package arrived for Douglas at the hotel. Inside was a brand new Visor – with complete instructions on how to transfer data from the old Visor into the new one, as well as a pre-addressed courier delivery slip.

All Douglas had to do was transfer his data, put the old Visor with the chipped cover into the box, apply the pre-printed label and then call the toll-free number to arrange an immediate courier pick-up.

Douglas is clear and expressive about his feelings: 'This was truly delightful service. I define delightful as something completely beyond the expected, something that brings joy to the customer. And I certainly received it in this case. I give a big hand of applause to Handspring!'

Key Learning Point

When things go wrong, you have a precious opportunity to completely 'Wow!' your customer. Do everything you can to solve the problem in a fast, generous and very convenient manner.

Handspring understands the value of a truly delighted customer. Do you?

Action Steps

What is a truly delighted customer worth to your business in repeat sales, active referrals and positive word-of-mouth? Do your policies reflect this understanding? Do you actively make the investment required? Does everyone in your company agree?

1,500 puzzle pieces...minus one!

Vincent bought a 1,500-piece jigsaw puzzle from Robinson's Department Store for his wife. He writes:

'After spending two months on the puzzle, she was upset to find a last piece missing. We searched the house but the piece eluded us. At our wits' end, we went to Robinson's for help.

'To our great surprise, the staff, without asking another question, simply opened a new box of the same puzzle and assisted us in searching for our missing piece. Today, we are loyal shoppers at Robinson's – need I say more?'

Imagine the scene as Vincent, his wife and the sales staff pored through 1,500 pieces to find the missing piece. Imagine the feeling of intent collaboration as they sorted through the pieces by color and shape. Imagine the shared excitement when they finally 'found' the missing piece.

Imagine how many shoppers noticed this effort and gained a positive impression of the store's after-sales service.

Imagine the satisfaction felt by Vincent's wife as she put the missing piece into place. Imagine how much money Vincent and his wife will spend at Robinson's this year.

It would have been *easier* for Robinson's to simply give a whole new puzzle! Easier, yes, but much less effective from a customer loyalty point of view.

Key Learning Point

When things go wrong, your best *recovery effort* is required. But don't just provide the missing piece (that's the recovery), also provide unique personal assistance (*that* is the memorable effort).

Action Steps

Give your staff the authority they need to take immediate recovery actions. Speed and generosity get remembered and rewarded.

Laundry Unlimited 'bounces back'

We use a convenient laundry service that picks up our dry-cleaning and delivers.

A new pair of fashion pants came back from the cleaner utterly destroyed. The cloth had bubbled and buckled and almost torn apart.

Next to the telephone number on the laundry receipt was a small note: 'Liability may be limited to the cost of dry-cleaning.'

With concern in my voice, I called the proprietor of Laundry Unlimited. To her credit, she listened to my report and immediately replied, 'Well, it sounds like we need to buy you another pair of pants without delay.'

Dry-cleaning cost? $7. New pants? $150.

It will take many dry-cleanings for Laundry Unlimited to earn back the money spent replacing our pants. But Linda has earned our loyalty for many years to come.

She deserves the profits she will make.

Key Learning Point

When things go wrong, don't hesitate to *spend money* setting things right. It isn't money spent at all; it's money wisely invested.

Action Steps

What is the 'cash value' of things that break, malfunction, get lost or otherwise go awry for your customers? Are you ready to spend that amount – immediately – to set things right?

For a lifetime of customer loyalty, are you willing to invest even more?

Preserve the loyalty you deserve

My videotape duplication company has been a reliable and responsive supplier. They should be – I have spent more than $62,000 with them in the past few years.

I received a complaint from a customer about one of my videotapes that 'skipped' during playback. I thought it was an oddity and immediately replaced the tape. But the next month another complaint arrived about the same situation.

I contacted the duplication company right away. They explained this problem may have affected a small number of videocassettes from a single spool of defective tape. They apologized profusely and promised immediate replacement. I removed all remaining inventory from my office and sent the tapes back, a few hundred pieces from the most recent batch of duplications.

Then I got a message from the company offering to replace only 'verified bad tapes', and not *all* the tapes I had returned.

What am I supposed to do, watch every tape and look out for those that 'skip'? Or wait for my customers to notice the problem and complain, and then exchange those tapes one at a time? Of course not.

The better course of action is to simply – and quickly – replace them all. I told them so in a follow-up message.

To their credit, the duplication company responded to my second message in an entirely appropriate manner. They have agreed to replace all the tapes promptly and at no charge.

They also promise to put extraordinary care into my future duplications to ensure the highest quality standards.

That's a smart business move. It guarantees another $62,000.

Key Learning Point

When the service you provide jeopardizes your customer's relationship with their customers, you need to respond with twice the speed and twice the recovery effort. After all, now your upset customer has upset customers!

Of course there will be costs and consequences and perhaps some aggravation, but leap to it right away. Be the supplier who takes immediate action to set the wrong things right.

Action Steps

Who are your customers' customers? How do your actions as a supplier impact your customers' customers' satisfaction? If things go wrong, how will your response and recovery affect theirs?

Meet with your customers to discuss this on a regular basis. Develop a clear understanding and positive action plans. Make sure your customers, and your customers' customers, are well served.

Managing customer complaints

Managing customer complaints is a vital, internal process influencing customer perceptions and the attitudes of your staff.

Is your 'complaint management system' up-to-date? Use this checklist to review your current approach and, if needed, make it better.

1. Focus on the complaint

Read the complaint with an open and appreciative mind. Complaints are an opportunity to fix problems and prevent them from re-occurring.

Identify the 'value dimension' your customer is complaining about. A value dimension is that aspect of the service interaction your customer truly values, but which has been under-delivered or unfulfilled.

Value dimensions are always positive, often the opposite of your customer's complaint. For example, if they complain about slow response, the value dimension is speed. If they complain about rude staff, the value dimension is respect, courtesy and staff attitude.

2. Focus on the company

Connect with those inside your organization who can make improvements in the identified value dimensions. This may be people responsible for procedures, staff development, etc.

Study the complaint with your team and determine what should be changed or improved to prevent repetition.

Confirm who will make the changes required. Be clear about who will do what and by when.

Track customer complaints in this value dimension over time.

3. Focus on the customer

Assess the impact of this problem on your customer. Has your customer been severely pained or is the impact minor? Is your customer cool, or hot and ready to explode?

Plan the actions needed to set things right for this customer. Express empathy and apologize. Give an explanation of what will be improved inside the company. Prepare specific positive actions. Include a generous gesture of goodwill to demonstrate your appreciation.

Then contact the customer by phone, e-mail, letter or in person. Make them *feel* right by agreeing on the importance of the value dimension they hold so dear. Tell them how committed you are to improving this dimension of your service and to reclaiming their full satisfaction.

Explain the specific actions you plan to take on their behalf. Confirm whether these will be sufficient to restore your customer's confidence and trust.

After you have taken the actions, follow-through to be sure your customer is satisfied and intends to patronize you again.

Key Learning Point

Most people with a complaint won't even tell you about it. Instead, they'll walk away and tell other people: your customers, prospects and competitors – sometimes government agencies and the press!

Customers who do complain are actually your best friends, your free consultants, your valued business partners. Be sure you treat them that way.

Action Steps

Review, revise and reinforce your complaints management policy and procedures. Make sure every upset customer becomes a happy customer.

Manage positive comments, too! When you receive a customer compliment, send an appreciative and informative reply. Turn your happy customers into bona fide ambassadors: eager to return, willing to stay in touch, ready to promote you with positive word-of-mouth.

Track each complaint until your customer comes back

When you respond to a customer complaint, what do you hope will happen next? In many cases, the answer is 'nothing'.

But when you reply and the result is silence, have you genuinely resolved the issue? Is your customer truly satisfied? Or have they simply gone quiet, and maybe gone away?

If you're making a sincere effort to respond to customer complaints, then make sure you also track complaining customers until you are absolutely *sure* they have come back.

If you run a restaurant, make sure they come back for dinner. If you work in travel, be sure they come back on board. If you're in a bank, check they're still using their credit cards. If not, your recovery effort remains incomplete.

My friend Steven Howard puts it this way: 'A customer is not a customer until she buys from you the *second* time. The first time she is only a "trial user". The second time she becomes a "customer". The third time she qualifies as a "repeat customer" and, over time, may become truly loyal.'

Key Learning Point

Complaining customers are more active and vocal than most. Your response should not shut them up, it should win them back.

Action Steps

Start tracking the return and repeat purchases of your complaining customers. If they come back and patronize you again, you are on the road to great reward. If they go away and don't return, your 'complaint reply system' is not working as it should.

Follow up with complaining customers who do *not* return. Find out what you could have done, or should have done, to truly recover their business. Then implement their suggestions – and keep on tracking.

13

THE INFINITE
ABSURDITY AWARDS

'Don't let your worst service make
a fool of your company and you.'

Don't let your systems drive your customers crazy!

Does your company run like clockwork? Are your accountants pleased with how everything moves smoothly? Are your managers content with how customers are managed by your system?

If so, watch out! Your present methods, regulations, policies and procedures may be convenient for the company but utterly frustrating for your customers.

Customers discover these landmines of dissatisfaction almost by accident, stumbling upon them in the normal course of business. Dedicated customers will speak up and complain. Others will just go away.

I am a customer who makes a point of letting companies know when their policies are frustrating, preposterous or just plain customer-unfriendly.

Unfortunately, many organizations have built up a thick layer of resistance and defensiveness towards such feedback. They have stopped listening to the voice of the customer...especially the customer with a complaint.

Sometimes I wonder whether anyone is listening at all.

The stories in this book are all true, and many are entertaining. But they are only valuable if they inspire you to listen more closely to your customers and to more carefully examine your policies and procedures.

Key Learning Point

Customers are often frustrated by standardized and inflexible policies. This may cause your customers to fume in frustration, but the rest of your staff and system may quietly conspire to silence the voice of complaining customers. You have to make an effort to really *listen*.

Action Steps

Ask your customers:

'How can we serve you better? What frustrates you most about the way we provide our service? Is there anything you would like us to do more of? less of? start doing? stop doing? What do other companies do for you that we don't do here?'

Ask your staff:

'What do our customers ask for that frustrates you the most? Are there any special customer requests that drive you crazy? Is there anything they ask for that is against our company policy?'

Ask your managers:

'Is it the customers that make our staff so mad, or are they driven to distress by limitations in our systems, policies and procedures?'

Ask other service providers:

Whenever you dine, travel, shop, purchase or rent, make special requests. Ask for things that are 'not on the menu', slightly different from the routine.

Watch carefully how each establishment responds. Are they fast, flexible and friendly? What is it about their policy and systems that allows them to respond that way?

Learn to improve your own systems by testing the flexibility of others.

Finally, ask yourself:

Are you willing to make the changes your customers require?

Your accountant and your managers may be comfortable. But who are you in business for?

Your Accounting Department will still be with you tomorrow. Will your customers be with you, too?

The conference rate in Los Angeles

I was making arrangements to attend a conference in Los Angeles, California.

As a frequent flyer, I receive award coupons offering a 50% discount from normal hotel rates. I contacted the call center of a major hotel chain to make my reservation.

The reservations clerk was friendly and very helpful. She took my name and contact numbers. She confirmed the dates, my room preference and credit card number. She asked if I was a 'Premium Club' member, which I was not. So she registered me for Club status over the phone.

Then she remarked, 'Mr. Kaufman, now that you *are* a Premium Club member, I can offer you an even lower rate for an upgraded room on a higher floor. And a fruit basket will be waiting for you upon arrival.'

I was surprised and delighted. My special room rate was just $100 per night.

Signing off from this great telephone experience, I said: 'Thank you for your help. I am looking forward to staying at the hotel during the conference.'

'The conference?', she quickly replied, 'What conference are you attending?'

When I told her about the event, she said, 'Oh. If you are attending that conference, you have to use our conference rate of $124.'

I laughed and assured her I was happy with the special rate and Club status she had already confirmed.

'Oh no,' she repeated. 'If you are coming for the conference, you must use the special rate. We have a block of rooms already reserved for you on a lower floor. And I'm afraid you don't get the fruit basket.'

A lower floor, higher rate and no fruit basket? I protested.

But my protest was in vain. She checked with her supervisor, who concurred. 'I'm sorry, but that's our policy,' she said without much concern.

I surrendered to her insistence, listened sadly as she cancelled my Premium Club reservation, but declined to have her book me back into the hotel at the higher conference rate. I hung up the phone in disbelief.

Then I called right back and reached a different reservations clerk and made another reservation, again using my frequent flyer award coupon and my new Premium Club membership number. This time I kept my mouth shut about attending any conference.

I paid $100 per night when I went to Los Angeles. I enjoyed the Towers room and a complimentary fruit basket upon arrival. No thanks, though, to this hotel's absurd policy and customer-unfriendly procedures.

Somewhere deep within the marketing department of this hotel chain, yield-management professionals carefully calculate the maximum rate they can squeeze from participants at each international conference.

Meanwhile conference participants are also thinkers…real, live customers! Yield managers, are you listening?

Key Learning Point

When your policies cross, collide or contradict, your customers will find out. Clean up the confusion!

Action Steps

Review the many ways your customers can confirm, order, book, engage, hire, rent or purchase your products and service. Look for mismatches and inconsistencies in the policies and procedures. Get them back in line so your company and your customers stay aligned.

Hertz Rent-a-Car in San Francisco

I wanted to make a three-day car reservation for a visit to San Francisco.

I called Hertz Rent-a-Car, where I am a member of the 'Hertz Number One Club' for frequent travelers. I planned to use an award coupon for one free-day rental from American Airlines and additional award coupons for two more free days from United Airlines.

The telephone reservations officer provided impeccable service. She greeted me pleasantly, acknowledged me as a member of the Hertz Number One Club, confirmed my dates, flights, pick-up location and choice of automobile.

Then she asked me what time I would be returning the car after the first day of rental. 'I want the car for all three days,' I replied.

'You can't keep the same car for all three days,' she asserted. 'After the first day you have to bring the car back and pick up a different car for the next two days. The first day is paid for with your American Airlines coupon, but the next two days are paid for with your United coupons.'

'So what's the difference?', I responded. 'I am the same person, with the same Hertz Number One Club member. I am the rightful owner of both the award coupons, and I want a Hertz automobile for three consecutive days. Surely you will let me keep the same car, so I don't have to come back to the airport in the middle of my Bay Area vacation.'

'That's not the way our system works here, Mr. Kaufman,' she replied.

'But it *should* work that way, don't you agree?', I asked, appealing to her sense of elementary logic, simple concern and practical customer care.

'I don't make the rules here, Mr. Kaufman. I just follow them. What time will you be returning the car after the first day?'

Somewhere within the heart of Hertz, a group of senior rule-makers live comfortably with their precise policy of 'one airline, one coupon, one car, no exceptions'.

But somewhere close to this customer's heart lies frustration, inconvenience and incredible disbelief.

I'm not the type of customer who gives up in these situations. When my first 'one-day' reservation began, I had a long chat with the most senior Hertz rental manager I could find. He let me keep the same car for all three days.

Someone at Hertz Rent-A-Car was listening.

Key Learning Point

Elementary logic and practical customer care are the best rules to use in many situations. At Nordstroms clothing store, famous for excellent service, they simply tell the staff: 'The rule is to use your common sense. There are no other rules.'

Action Steps

If your rules and regulations don't make sense to your customers, they need to be rewritten. If you can see logic where your customers cannot, it's not your customers' sight that needs refocusing.

You can't have juice with a Special Broiler Meal

Years ago, I frequented a well-known quick-service restaurant for their Special Broiler Meal, a fast-food lunch of broiled chicken sandwich and french fries.

But instead of taking the large cola with the package, I always asked for a small glass of orange juice instead. Predictably, the counter staff would freeze up with uncertainty and refer my request to the floor manager.

One young manager was particularly memorable. 'I'm sorry, sir,' he told me. 'You can't have orange juice with the Special Broiler Meal.'

'Sure I can,' I replied, 'I do it all the time at the other outlets in your group. There is a 65 cent price difference and I am happy to pay it.'

'That's not the problem,' he said with a touch of annoyance. 'There's no key on my computer to make the substitution, so I can't let you do it.'

'Hey, sometimes you have to break the rules,' I said, reminding him of his brand's multi-million dollar advertising campaign. 'I'll take the Super Broiler Meal, with orange juice, please.'

He realized I was not going to take 'No' for an answer and he could not go against a well-informed customer and his chain's well-known advertising promise.

'I'll do it for you just this once, as an exception,' he said.

'Oh c'mon, you can do it for me anytime,' I replied.

'No,' he said again, looking me straight in the eye. 'I will do it for you this once, but I won't do it again.'

'Wait a minute,' I asked gamely. 'You are about to make me a happy customer. Do you really mean you wouldn't make me a happy customer again?'

'I will do it for you this once,' he repeated flatly. When I received my meal, with orange juice, I gave the manager a genuine smile and said, 'See you again next time.'

He replied, just below his breath but loud enough for me to hear, 'I don't want to see you again.'

Somewhere within this company, computer programmers design point-of-purchase terminals to carefully limit the choices and options of customers around the world.

The accountants are happy. Daily sales reports are clean and accurate. But at the sales counter, face-to-face between customers and staff, both parties experience frustration.

The advertising slogan says, 'Sometimes you've just got to break the rules.' But the restaurant manager would not.

I wrote an article about this encounter in my local newspaper. The following week, a regional manager from the restaurant chain called and invited me to lunch.

The next month I returned to the same outlet seeking a Super Broiler Meal, with orange juice. The counter staff smiled brightly and keyed in my order.

'How did you do that?', I asked in a state of pleased amazement. 'Now it's easy,' she replied. 'Last week they put a new key on the computer to allow simple menu changes.'

Congratulations to this well-known restaurant chain. You are listening!

Key Learning Point

If you are going to bend the rules for your customers, be ready to do it each and every time they ask. Then make life easier for them, and for you – change the procedure, or change the rules.

Action Steps

Some rules are essential and must be maintained. Others should be refined or abandoned. Try suspending a different rule each week. Notice what new actions can be taken, new customer value created. Then keep the rules you really need and get rid of those you don't.

Doing right – or doing better?

I arrived at the airport early. The check-in agent was very polite, but also concerned. Despite my confirmed Business Class ticket, the airline had no record of my reservation, and Business Class was already fully booked.

I asked if seats were available in First Class. The agent said 'Yes'.

'No problem,' I smiled. 'How about an upgrade into one of the empty seats upfront?' She smiled back, but did not issue a boarding pass.

Twenty minutes later I was still standing nervously at the counter while two staff members double-checked the computer, spoke at length with my travel agent on the phone and then called their manager for instructions.

Again I said politely, 'I have been a qualified frequent flyer with your airline for the past five years in a row. Surely you can provide a bit of special treatment by upgrading me into one of the empty seats in First Class.'

The staff replied sincerely, 'We will definitely do an upgrade, Mr. Kaufman. But there are other passengers seated in Business Class who have even more years of frequent flyer qualification than you do. The person with highest seniority will move up to First Class.'

'Wait a minute,' I replied. 'The passenger with "highest seniority" has no idea a problem even exists. I am sure he would enjoy moving up to First Class, but he's probably quite content where he is right now in Business Class.

'I, on the other hand, arrived at your check-in counter with a confirmed Business Class ticket to find you show no reservation in my name. I've watched for twenty minutes while you and your colleagues try to sort this out. I've been delayed at check-in, and I am completely aware of the current problem. And now you tell me that you are going to upgrade a passenger who has no concern, no problem, and no complaint? This makes no sense. The passenger you upgrade should be me!'

She knew my suggestion was right but replied quietly, 'It's the company policy.' And company policy prevailed. Unintentionally, the airline added insult to inconvenience.

The passenger who was upgraded to First Class had seven years of frequent flyer qualification; I had five.

On board I read the airline's in-flight magazine. An article announced the airline's brand new customer service initiative. It said, 'We are talking about empowering frontline service staff to seize service opportunities as they arise... A more personalized and innovative service will be possible through a flexible approach to systems and procedures.'

After the flight, the airline did explain its policy to me in great detail, but did nothing more to soothe the pain. 'Talking about' is not the same as doing.

I remain a loyal customer of this airline, praising them often in my speeches around the world. But I am also keen to help them improve and grow.

When they deserve the praise, I say it. When they need constructive feedback, I send it in. You should do the same.

Key Learning Point

It is not enough just to make announcements and speeches and launch new service campaigns. You must give your people the power to do the *right* thing, not just the right policy thing.

Action Steps

Learn to see the world from your customers' point of view. Truly empower your staff. Allow them to make customer-friendly decisions when they know it's the right thing to do.

Getting (dis)connected

 My friend purchased a desk-top publishing computer from a major online computer hardware vendor.

She ordered the powerful stand-alone workstation configured just the way she wanted, with a large monitor, big hard disk and high-speed graphics card. At the same time, she purchased a top-of-the-line scanner and laser printer.

When the components arrived, she could not find the cable to connect her computer with the printer. Naturally, she was concerned and called the vendor. The vendor told her she should *buy* a cable from a local computer shop.

That's absurd! If she wanted to go shopping for computer parts, she might as well buy the whole system from her local vendor.

People buy online for convenience, not to be sent shopping locally for missing cables.

My friend protested.

The vendor told her to carefully read the packing slip enclosed with her new laser printer, and pointed out that a cable for connecting the printer with a computer was *not* included on the list.

That's absurd, too! The vendor may be right about what's not included with a printer, but they were completely wrong about solving her very real problem.

My friend protested again.

At which point the vendor tried to justify *why* no cable was provided.

The vendor explained that many customers now buy laser printers for installation in 'networked environments' where the required connecting cables are already provided.

That's absurdity of the highest order!

The vendor *knew* my friend bought a stand-alone system

because the very same vendor sold, assembled and delivered the stand-alone computer to her.

Let me clarify that I admire this computer manufacturer and vendor enough to own their machines – and their stock. However, at this point in the story I became personally involved and wrote directly to the company.

For their persistent justification, bureaucratic inflexibility and blatant unwillingness to see the world from their customer's point of view, this major online computer vendor became the dubious recipient of an 'Infinite Absurdity Award'.

Two days later, the vendor shipped my friend the connecting cable she required. They had cables in stock all along.

Key Learning Point

Convenience is a great value to offer your customers, especially in today's busy world. But convenience is measured by your *customer's* experience, not by your explanations, justifications or packing lists. The smallest missing item can become a big customer problem.

Action Steps

Consider *every* aspect of your customers' experience from the moment they order, to the time they receive, install, use, maintain, upgrade and replenish your product or service. Create new ways to smooth and streamline the process. Make it so *easy* for customers to do business with you that they don't even consider going to someone else.

Your goodwill has expired

Alice's prepaid telephone calling card said 'Expires August 31, 2001' on the back.

She decided to use the remaining value of the card at 8:00 pm on August 31.

Unfortunately, the card had already been terminated when she tried to make a call. There was no value remaining. She held a worthless piece of plastic.

The telephone company had terminated her phone card's value on the very *first minute* of the listed expiration date (12:01 am), rather than the very last minute as Alice had expected (11:59 pm).

The company may be technically right, but commercially they are dead wrong.

When you see an expiration date, don't you assume the product is valid until the *end* of that date? Isn't that how your credit card works? Isn't that how a food expiration date works? Isn't that how your telephone calling card should work, too?

Key Learning Point

When setting policies and procedures, make every effort to see the world from your customer's point of view. Make *their* view, *your* view.

Action Steps

Carefully review all recent customer complaints. Look for cases where customers complain that your policies are too narrow, your processes too slow or your procedures too bureaucratic.

Revisit the source of these complaints. Is there another way to see the situation? Do your customers have a point you should consider? Start making changes. Keep on improving until *their* views and *your* views are aligned.

We are really sorry for you, but...

WE'RE **NOT** SO SORRY

I lost my mobile telephone. The telephone company told me to file a police report and then come down to their office to buy a new phone.

When I arrived, the counter staff member was helpful and understanding. She gave me a discount on my new phone purchase and a free replacement SIM card holding my personal account details. I was pleased and grateful.

Five months later I lost my handphone again! This time I knew what to do. I filed a new police report and went back to the company to buy a new phone.

The counter staff member was helpful and understanding, but she gave me neither a discount on the new phone nor a free replacement SIM card. I asked if she had forgotten, or if the company policy had changed.

She replied, 'We are very sorry that you lost the phone, and our policy is to give a discount and a free SIM card to make things a little easier for you. But our records show you lost your phone five months ago, and we can only feel sorry for you once a year.'

Key Learning Point

Generosity is a good service policy *whenever* your customers need help. If they need help twice, be generous twice. (No one loses their mobile phone twice on purpose...)

Action Steps

Look for situations where your company policy restricts the flow of generosity towards customers who have a problem. Change the policy. Don't hold back. Give generously when customers need you. Over time they will reward you.

But everybody knows about it

I recently stayed at a major hotel in Perth, Australia. On the telephone in my room was a small card indicating the phone and fax numbers of the hotel.

The phone number was listed as (09)225-1234.

Clients around the world intended to call me during my stay, so I gave them the hotel number.

Not a single person was able to reach me by phone. One sent e-mail complaining I had given him a wrong number.

I called the hotel operator to check the telephone number and told her about the small card in my room.

'Oh,' she replied, 'the local code is not (09) anymore, now it's (08).'

'When did that change?' I asked.

'About four years ago,' she replied, 'but everyone knows about it.'

I quickly contacted my clients overseas, and gave them the new number to reach me (08)225-1234.

Again, not a single person was able to reach me by phone! I received another wave of 'wrong number' complaints.

I called the hotel operator a second time, again reading her the phone number on the card in my room, but changing (09) to (08).

'Oh,' she replied again, 'the code *is* (08), but now you also have to keep the 9 as part of the main phone number.'

'So the correct number is actually (08)9225-1234,' I confirmed. 'When did that change?'

'About four years ago,' she replied, 'but everyone knows about it.'

Absurd, isn't it? This hotel has 367 rooms, and very few people staying overnight in those rooms come from Perth.

I wonder how many guests have experienced the same problem over the past four years? I wonder how many staff from Housekeeping and Rooms Division see, clean, straighten and even replenish those inaccurate little notecards *every day*?

I spoke with the Business Manager, Michelle. She thanked me for my feedback and promised to do something about it right away.

I asked her to post a $100 credit to my room account, not to compensate for my frustration, but to ensure the hotel took this matter seriously and would get the issue resolved. She agreed immediately and promised to make the adjustment on my bill.

The next morning when I checked out of the hotel, *no* credit posted to my account. How predictably inefficient.

I wonder if it will be four more years before the small cards in the rooms are changed? I wonder how many more guests will suffer with wrong telephone numbers posted in their rooms? I wonder how many times the hotel operator will say 'But everyone knows about it.'

Key Learning Point

Over time, many facts do change including phone numbers, features, stocking codes, availability, prices, procedures, packages, prerequisites and more. If you don't keep them up to date, your customers will find the errors, and feel the pain.

Action Steps

Check your data now. Be sure every piece of public information about your company, products and services is accurate and up to date.

When customers look, listen, read, research, surf, shop or ask questions, be sure the information they receive is current and complete, not old or obsolete.

Never on a sundae

I was passing through Kuala Lumpur International Airport (KLIA) in Malaysia, returning from a live webcast presentation on a new e-learning channel.

One of my small indulgences after a good presentation is the soft chocolate-and-vanilla swirled ice cream available at the quick service restaurant just before Immigration at KLIA.

A young staff member was at the ice-cream machine. I asked her for the vanilla-and-chocolate swirl in an ice-cream sundae cup with a squirt of chocolate syrup on top. (I don't have this very often, but when I do, I enjoy it.)

She said that I could only have the sundae with vanilla ice cream, not the vanilla and chocolate swirl. The three small nozzles for dispensing vanilla, chocolate and vanilla-and-chocolate were located side by side.

I asked again, very nicely, for her to use the vanilla-and-chocolate nozzle instead of the plain vanilla. Again, she declined. 'The sundae comes with vanilla,' she said, 'not with vanilla-and-chocolate.'

I'd had the sundae with vanilla-and-chocolate in the very same restaurant a few months earlier. I explained this to her and asked once more. Once again, she declined.

The store manager agreed with the staff: vanilla-and-chocolate ice cream was definitely not part of the sundae.

I pressed for a win–win solution. The manager said, 'You can buy the large ice cream cone in vanilla-and-chocolate, and then we can give you a plastic cup to put it in to make a sundae.'

'But what will I do with the ice-cream cone?' I wondered out loud.

Without a moment's pause she replied, 'You can throw it away.'

And that is exactly what we did.

I bought the large vanilla-and-chocolate ice-cream cone and the manager gave me the plastic cup for a sundae. I turned the vanilla-and-chocolate ice cream out of the cone and into the cup, and threw away the cone.

Then the young staff member politely put a squirt of chocolate syrup on top – exactly what I had wanted from the beginning.

But there was a bonus: the price of a sundae was $2.50, while the price of the large cone was only $1.60. They insisted on charging me only for the price of the large cone. Since they couldn't figure out what else to do, the plastic cup and squirt of chocolate syrup were free.

Key Learning Point

In a world where customer choice is only a nozzle away, staff must be given the authority and responsibility to make obvious decisions in favor of the customer, and the company. Rigid policies that limit choice and force staff into bizarre situations are the problem, not the staff, nor the cone, nor the nozzles.

Action Steps

What policies do you have in place that make your customers laugh (or cry)? What standards do your staff routinely run around? Is tighter adherence to standards and controls the best or only answer? It's a vanilla *and* chocolate world out there – make sure your staff and your policies adapt.

Developing an eye for detail

I flew Business Class on one of the world's largest airlines and found myself in a chair padded for pleasure.

This up-to-date seating boasts an impressive list of features: reclining back with adjustable lumbar support, extended leg rest, electronic 'rolling massage', adjustable headrest with padded wings, two reading lights, a power point for laptop computers, a telephone, Internet connection, special built-in pouch for personal effects, large video screen with 14 movie selections, 19 audio channels, and noise-canceling headphones.

I was so impressed, I decided to write some positive feedback for the airline on the spot. I asked the friendly cabin crew member for a 'comment card' and a pen.

She handed me a pen from her pocket that read 'Narita Tokyu Hotel' and said she would look for a comment card, but wasn't sure if there were any aboard.

She returned a few moments later and handed me an airline writing kit with three postcards, two envelopes, and two sheets of airline stationery in an attractive blue folder. And she confirmed there were no comment cards aboard.

I thought that was odd. Simple comment cards are cheap to print, easy to use, and fast to hand out and collect. The fancy writing kit costs the airline much more, yet it doesn't help solicit customer feedback.

Stranger still was the pen: 'Narita Tokyu Hotel'?

'Don't you have any *airline* pens?' I asked.

She blushed and replied 'No. We used to carry them, but we don't any more. But passengers still ask us for pens all the time, so we take extra ones from the hotels where we stay.'

'Really?!' I laughed. 'The airline installed these great new seats and hands out fancy writing kits, but doesn't carry inexpensive plastic pens on board for passenger use?'

She grinned sheepishly and brought me a sample of what the airline *does* provide for Business Class passengers who wish to write: a small *golf pencil*. About three inches long, these little blue pencils are sharp as a tack and emblazoned with the airline's name and logo in white.

I am sitting in a world-class airline seat. I can get a classy, expensive writing kit just by asking. But if I seek a ballpoint pen, the airline gives me a tiny pencil made for golf.

A cost-savings effort was to blame. The cabin crew explained that too many passengers kept asking for the pens.

How penny foolish! When a Business Class customer takes an airline pen home, that airline's name is seen every time the pen is used. An average pen lasts hundreds if not thousands of uses. In advertising terms, that's a lot of brand name impressions on the existing customer base.

But who gets all those valuable advertising impressions in this airline's case? The 'Narita Tokyu Hotel'!

Well, not quite. Another hour into the flight the same cabin crew member came back with a shy request, 'Excuse me, Mr. Kaufman. Can I have the pen back, please? Another passenger needs it...'

Key Learning Point

Be sure *your* products keep pace with industry improvements. Other airlines must take note of this airline's terrific seating. For long-haul flights in upper-class travel (where airline profits are made), seat enhancements do make a difference. But don't neglect the little things that make a difference to your customers.

Action Steps

Examine your product improvement budgets. Where are you spending? Where are you saving money? Will your customers notice the impact?

Lack of integration = customer frustration

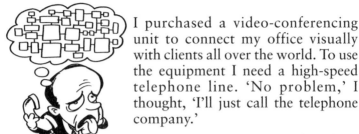 I purchased a video-conferencing unit to connect my office visually with clients all over the world. To use the equipment I need a high-speed telephone line. 'No problem,' I thought, 'I'll just call the telephone company.'

The telephone company referred me to the ISDN Department for high-speed access. The ISDN Department referred me to an outside vendor who faxed me an application form from the telephone company!

I filled out the forms and faxed them back to the vendor. He faxed them back to the ISDN Department, who then called me to arrange an appointment. But the appointment is only to 'lay the line'. A second appointment is needed after that to 'commission the line'. In between these two appointments, the vendor must come once again to install special 'terminator' equipment. Phew!

As I was ordering high-speed access for video-conferencing, I considered using the same line for high-speed access to the Internet. The vendor faxed me another form from a *different* department of the telephone company (the Internet Access Department), which I filled out and returned to the vendor. The vendor faxed the form to the Internet Access Department.

The Internet Access Department called me to clarify my decision. Was I aware of the extra charges? Did I know the line was not toll-free like my current analog line? Had the vendor explained that I needed yet another piece of special equipment. Phew!

I asked whether it was better to use ISDN for high-speed Internet access, or should I use ADSL (another type of high-speed service). The person from the Internet Access Department said I had to speak to the people in the ISDN Department for a comparison, but the lady at the ISDN Department didn't know anything about ADSL. In fact, she said, the ADSL Department was 'a different company'.

When I reached the ADSL Department (which is very much part of the same telephone company), I became quite overwhelmed trying to compare installation charges, monthly charges, toll vs. toll-free charges, monthly plans with hourly rates, and per minute charges above the monthly plans.

'And do you realize,' she asked, 'that you can use ISDN for videoconferencing and Internet access, but cannot use ADSL for Internet and video-conferencing without installation of another special server?' Phew!

No one at the telephone company could help me compare. The most helpful person was the outside vendor.

Finally, I gave up.

Key Learning Point

This telephone company desperately needs *one point of contact* to educate and serve customers in a user-friendly way. This single point of contact should be connected and empowered (internally and externally) to make all necessary arrangements for sales, installation, commissioning, selection of new equipment, scheduling of appointments, questions about billing...even customer training after installation, if required.

The critical issue is not cost. People are willing to pay for value-added services. The critical issue is convenience for the customer.

PS: This telephone company is about to get a major new competitor. Watch out!

Action Steps

Now look at *your* procedures and processes from your customers' point of view. If your system is disjointed, unclear or confusing, your customers are going to have a problem. Which means *you* have a problem, too!

Please drive around once again

In Australia, Matt and two friends went to a fast-food drive-through for lunch. They wanted three separate orders as there were three in the car and no one had exact change.

The order-taker replied, 'I'm sorry sir, but we are only allowed to process two drive-through orders at a time.'

'But there's no-one behind us,' they replied.

The order taker repeated, 'I'm sorry sir, but we are only allowed to process two drive-through orders at a time.'

The driver asked, 'You mean I can place two orders now, drive through and pick them up, then drive through again to get my last order?'

'That's right,' the order-taker said. 'If you want more than two orders please come inside or drive through again.'

So Matt and his friends drove around the building to place their third order. In the time it took them to drive around the building, not one other car appeared. It was a pretty small building.

Matt spoke to the manager on duty who repeated the same comments: 'Our owner wants a maximum of two orders per car so we don't slow down other customers.' A noble decision, perhaps, but with one big flaw: *there were no other customers waiting.*

Key Learning Point

Policies implemented for the good of the customers must be good for the customers, too.

Action Steps

Check your current policies in all areas of customer contact and concern. Look for lunacy, lost logic and loopholes. Make the changes required.

14

SOMETIMES SERVICE STINKS

'In the quest for superior service, sometimes we
encounter those who just don't understand.'

The cheesecake of tomorrow

At an elegant resort in Mauritius, the dessert menu was rather sparse. One customer asked the waiter for 'The Special Dessert of Today'.

The waiter returned from the kitchen and reported flatly, 'We only have the cheesecake of tomorrow.'

Nonplussed, the customer asked for further explanation.

'The Special of Today is sold out,' the waiter explained, 'We only have the cheesecake of tomorrow.'

'Well, can I have a piece of the cheesecake of tomorrow?' asked the guest.

'I suppose so,' replied the waiter, and brought this customer a piece of tomorrow's cheesecake – today.

Key Learning Point

What staff members *say* to your customers reveals a lot about how they are trained and what they consider to be possible, or important.

Action Steps

Use a mystery shopper (or be a mystery shopper). Visit your business in person and over the phone. Listen carefully to how your staff reply when asked a series of routine, unusual and penetrating questions. Train them to focus on customers' needs, not on policies, dates and procedures. Create satisfied customers today, or those customers may go elsewhere tomorrow.

Yes, we have no bananas

I stayed in an Orlando hotel suite for ten days. Breakfast was available in the concierge lounge each morning: oatmeal, bread with butter and jelly and an assortment of sliced melon.

Each morning I looked for a banana to top off my oatmeal. Sliced melon, yes. But banana, no.

On the third day I spoke to the staff in the lounge.

'You want a banana?' she asked. 'No problem. I'll have one for you tomorrow.'

The next morning, and every morning thereafter, she brought me a banana, usually keeping it hidden until I appeared. Occasionally another guest would see my special banana and look for another. But there were no more bananas. Only sliced melon.

Days later, I asked the Food & Beverage Manager, 'Why don't you provide bananas at breakfast? Other guests seem jealous of my bananas – and I notice the sliced melon is often sent back to the kitchen untouched.'

He replied, 'If we provide bananas, everyone would take one, or even two! That is more fruit than we want to give out in the morning. With the sliced melon, we know how much fruit we are allocating to the breakfast. Even if it is not eaten, we have control over our food costs.'

Our room rate on the Concierge Floor was more than $300 per night. Bananas cost about sixteen cents each.

Key Learning Point

If your staff have to bend the rules to keep your customers happy, it may be your rules that need revising.

Action Steps

Find a rule that gets bent regularly by your staff. Change the rule.

For just 30 cents of salad...

Simon sent me this lunchtime message:

'Whilst waiting for my toasted foccacia, a young man came into the shop and asked for a salad sandwich.

'While the shop owner prepared the sandwich, the young man kept saying "Give me heaps of carrot", and "Give me heaps of beetroot", etc.

'When it came time to pay, the shop owner rang up the transaction and said, "That's $3.50." The customer replied, "But the price says $3.20."

'The shop owner explained that the customer had requested "extra" salad. The customer was dismayed and replied, "I wasn't aware I had to pay extra."

'The shop owner became angry and stood his ground, insisting on the higher sandwich price. The customer said he did not have any more money and left with the shop owner giving him a filthy look.'

Of course, that customer will never return – and I'm quite sure he will tell others about his bad experience. Those he tells may avoid the sandwich shop, too.

The shop owner should have checked whether his menu pricing reflected a surcharge for 'extra' toppings. I looked, and it didn't.

For the sake of 30 cents, how much business has this shop owner lost?

It's quite true that customers will 'take advantage' every chance they get. But there's nothing wrong with that! In fact, it's why customers come to you in the first place. They have made their comparisons and decided that *you* offer best value for their money.

Why, then, should you be upset when customers try to get everything they can? After all, you offered it.

The problem is not the customer, it's the company that lacks clear and attractive communications.

A simple note on the sandwich shop menu reading 'Extra Items = 30 cents', would have neatly solved the problem.

What would solve the problem at *your* place of business?

Key Learning Point

Full-bodied communication with customers leads to understanding and delight. By contrast, sparse or misleading communication leads only to distress.

Action Steps

Do a complete review of your marketing materials, product and service guidelines, purchasing instructions and guarantees. Make sure every promise you make is crystal clear, and everything you offer is completely and gladly delivered.

The holidays are here

I use a credit card for many business purchases. Since I travel a lot, this means quite a bit of money is charged throughout the year.

Therefore, I was pleased when my bank had a local hotel deliver a 'basket of goodies' to our home during the holidays.

The card attached thanked us for our support, and looked forward to another year of providing beneficial service.

Unfortunately, the basket included abalone, chocolate cake and cookies. I am vegetarian (no abalone), we don't eat chocolate (no cake), and we try to avoid too much sugar (bye-bye cookies).

I'm sure the hotel has other options: nuts, flowers, a voucher for dinner – any of which I would have appreciated more.

In fact, I would have loved a phone call saying, 'Hello Mr. Kaufman. On behalf of your bank, we would like to send you a gift of your choice. Would you like wine, chocolate cake and cookies? Or would you prefer nuts and a large bouquet of flowers? Or perhaps a voucher for dinner at one of our fine restaurants? Or shall we donate the cash value to a charity of your choice?'

The cost to the bank would have been the same. The difference would be a phone call…and the desire to give customers what they want, not what you think they should want.

Key Learning Point

Don't assume you know what your customer really wants. Find out. It doesn't take much effort: just a phone call, and the right desire.

Action Steps

Before launching your next customer promotion, call your customers *first* and ask them what they think. Then, give them what they want.

A hard taste from a soft drink

Yusry in Dubai wrote: 'I had the pleasure of attending a popular cricket match. The event was sponsored by one of the major cola drinks.

'Unfortunately the day was marred by officials refusing to let my wife and me into the grounds. The reason for the refusal was that our carefully prepared bag of food and drink included a bottle that was not the sponsor's product.

'There were no warnings on our tickets that these products were not allowed. After arguing with the officials for some minutes, we were let into the grounds with our "illegal" bottle of cola. I hope the sponsor realizes that people do not enjoy such bully-boy tactics.'

With a bit of foresight, this negative experience could have been turned into a very positive moment.

Instead of banning the competitor's cola, the sponsor should have equipped and trained gate officials to say:

'Since the sponsor is generously supporting this event, may we replace your drinks for you for *free*? We'll be pleased to give you *two* bottles of delicious sponsor cola in exchange for each single bottle you have with you.'

The gate officials would feel prepared and generous. The customers would feel like they'd won an unexpected prize. And everyone would feel better about the sponsor.

Key Learning Point

Life is filled with unique situations. Think ahead. Overcome potential negatives with positive, creative and generous ideas. Don't leave a bad taste in your customer's mouth.

Action Steps

What could go *wrong* with your next project or promotion? Think ahead and plan what you will do to generously set things right.

Customer recovery first, system recovery second!

I was staying at a dive resort in Papua New Guinea recently. It was quite pleasant, with friendly staff, comfortable accommodation and good food.

I enjoyed a night dive with hungry starfish, scurrying crabs and parrot fish asleep amidst the coral. After the dive, however, I realized someone had slipped into my cabin and scurried off with a pair of pants and a matching canvas belt.

I did not sleep well and next morning reported the loss to the resort manager. 'Oh dear, we do have that problem,' she said. 'Are you sure you locked your door?' I assured her that I had, to which she replied, 'I guess we need to change the lock on that cabin.'

And that was it. From my point of view, someone had entered my room and helped themselves to my clothing. From her point of view, 'We need to change the lock.'

No apology. No offer to replace the lost clothing. No complimentary waiver of fees.

I did no more diving at that resort (who knows what else might scurry off?) and left a few days early.

Key Learning Point

When something goes wrong for your customer, you may know right away what needs to be done. But before you fix or change the system, set your precious customer at ease. Remember, there is a personal side to every breakdown. It's the side your customer feels first.

Action Steps

Be sure your service recovery plan takes care of your customer's feelings and emotions first, and fixes your system second.

Where on the floor is 264?

One of my students was looking for his room on the second floor of his hotel in London, United Kingdom.

The corridor was being renovated and all the wall signs had been taken down. The guest saw a member of the hotel staff and asked, 'Where can I find room 264?'

The staff thought for a moment and replied, 'Between room 263 and 265,' and then walked off.

It took the customer a moment to realize the absurdity of what he had just heard. By the time he turned for better guidance, the staff member was gone.

Key Learning Point

Your customers may require more than technical data to fulfill their wants and needs. Data only becomes useful information when it connects with human concerns.

Action Steps

Give your customers support, coaching, application guidelines, hand-holding, respect, encouragement and practical, useful advice. Make sure they get what they need: assistance, not just answers.

Customers...NO!

We were visiting in Gisborne, an attractive small town near Melbourne, Australia.

Walking along the main street I saw a small clothing store with a very bold sign pasted on the door directly above the doorknob. It read:

CUSTOMERS NO...
jam donuts, sticky buns, fizzy drinks, mucky boots, cigarettes, ice creams, gooey lollies, water pistols, fairy floss or half-eaten fruit in this shop. Thank you.

I understand the need to keep a shop clean, but the largest, loudest and strongest message in the sign is clearly:

CUSTOMERS NO...

In the window next to the door was an even larger sign:

UP TO 50% OFF!!

What an odd way to do business! The first sign scares customers away. The second begs them to come back by slashing prices (and profits).

Key Learning Point

Customers form opinions about every aspect of your business: your place, people, products, packaging and procedures. Anything not 100% customer friendly is a message that screams (or whispers): 'Stay Away!'

Action Steps

What messages are you sending to your clients? Review your website, application forms, product information, customer service counters, returns procedures, etc. Actively seek out moments that are unpleasant, inconvenient, problematic, confusing, offensive or difficult to understand. Then go to work and smooth the way. Make sure every point of contact says it loud and clear: CUSTOMERS WELCOME!

How to be customer unfriendly

One of my favorite airlines committed a customer interface blunder. They changed the automated telephone menu system for reservations, removed the 24-hour fast-access option for frequent flyers, set up the menu so it changes at various times of the day, and put long recorded messages on the system to 'educate' passengers while they wait.

I've called this airline many times. My fingers know which buttons to push to get what I need without delay. Now my fingers are lost, my ears are listening to long messages. I am still trying to figure out which menu works at which time of day and which buttons I need to push.

A similar experience took place when WordPerfect 5.0 introduced 'WordPerfect for Windows' and *all* the function keys were changed. Before that, WordPerfect 5.0 was *the* word-processing program of choice. (Remember the all-blue screen?)

Overnight my loyalty to WordPerfect evaporated. As long as I had to re-learn a whole new set of keystrokes, I might as well learn Microsoft Word. (You may have done the same.) What happened to WordPerfect? Massive decline in market share. We all know what's happening with Word.

Key Learning Point

Revolutionary transformation can have great power – but evolutionary change may keep your customers happier and profitably on board.

Action Steps

When you want to make a change or an 'upgrade' to your systems, keep your customer's experience foremost in your mind. Once your customers learn to love you, do all you can to keep them. Don't throw that love away!

Are you referable?

Technical competence alone does not make you 'referable', no matter how good you are.

My friend Treva recently experienced a car breakdown in Los Angeles. Her vehicle was towed to a nearby service station where the manager put her at ease with his comfortable style and obvious expertise. He promised to call her the next morning with an evaluation and an estimate.

She took the bus home. The next morning, he did not call. She called him in the afternoon. He apologized and agreed to call her back by the end of the day. But he didn't. She reached him again the next morning. This time he promised to call back within 45 minutes. Two hours later, he still had not called.

In the end, Treva's car was very well repaired. The manager gave her a clear explanation of what had gone wrong and charged her a very reasonable price.

I asked if she would take her car to this person in the future. She paused and replied, 'Yes. I can trust him to take good care of my car. But I won't refer him to anyone else. I can't trust him to take good care of my friends or my colleagues.'

Key Learning Point

Being technically competent is not enough to build a growing business. You may be a terrific lawyer, doctor, accountant, broker, supplier, programmer, manufacturer or car mechanic, but if you don't keep your promises in every way, you just won't be referred.

Action Steps

Promises are the foundation of reputation. Make them, and keep them.

Turtles deliver the internal mail

 The Corporate Events Manager at a leading high tech firm requested one of my demonstration videotapes.

I sent it promptly by Federal Express. Later, I checked the FedEx website (www.fedex.com) to track progress. The site provides instantaneous information, telling me my package was delivered at 9:27 am the very next day. Two days later I sent an e-mail to the manager, asking for her feedback on the video.

'I haven't received it yet,' she wrote back. 'We have Turtle Mail inside this company. I should get your package by the end of the week.'

Amazing! Federal Express picks up, delivers and tracks packages at warp speed...but inside this Fortune 500 company, the mailroom can't route an express package to the right desk within 48 hours!

Key Learning Point

From satellites to sanitation, the need for speed applies. What's the slowest part of your organization? Check it out, then *speed it up*!

Action Steps

Audit internal response times throughout your organization. How long does it take to route a package, reply to an e-mail, return a voice mail message? Identify bottlenecks that slow you down. Develop ways to speed things up and implement the solutions.

Who's answering your e-mail?

Websites, e-mail and digital voice mail are changing the game in business. Some companies are taking the lead with great digital service like Computers.com and Amazon.com. Others are falling far behind.

A friend of mine had a complaint about the service at a local hotel. He visited the hotel's website and wrote to the 'feedback' e-mail address provided.

One week later he got this reply:

'Dear Mr _____,

Sorry, but I'm not the PR manager. For an effective complaint letter, I suggest you write directly to our General Manager. He'll take immediate action. (Personally, I agree that the service here isn't fantastic.) Please do not mention my name in the letter. Thank you.'

Obviously the General Manager had no idea who was answering the hotel e-mail, or how it was being answered! (He does now. I forwarded him the message, without the writer's name.)

E-mail is just as important as a handwritten letter or a fax...only faster. Align your speed of response to the technology your customers are using.

Key Learning Point

Customers will communicate in whatever manner is most convenient for them. Provide high quality response at *every* point of contact and reply.

Action Steps

Ensure someone qualified answers all incoming e-mails. Have a standby in case that person is away. Impose a maximum response time of 24 hours, or sooner. E-mail doesn't wait!

How not to build with bytes

I bought a new notebook computer and wanted to get a 128-megabyte flash card for 'on the road' backups.

I sent an e-mail to the address listed on the business card of the store where I bought the computer. Explaining that I wanted to make an immediate purchase, I asked for their best price and delivery terms.

That was six weeks ago. Until today, no reply. And this store sells state-of-the-art computers!

So I bought the flash card somewhere else.

I had to wonder, how much more business is this computer store losing simply because the staff do not read and reply to e-mail?

Key Learning Point

What image is presented by putting an e-mail address on your business card? What image is created by not answering your mail?! People who use e-mail expect a speedy reply. Do it!

Action Steps

Benchmark e-mail response times of leading companies in your industry. Write to several firms and see how long it takes for them to reply. Then set a standard for your own firm that leads the field.

15

FINAL THOUGHTS

'I love the joy of being in touch, connecting us in service.'

What level of service do you provide?

We recently escaped to a fancy resort for a weekend of relaxation.

In the lobby we were welcomed by a staff member with a clipboard. He asked if we wanted our breakfast delivered to our room in the morning, or if we planned to eat at the restaurant. We had just arrived. We had not decided. He seemed a bit perplexed.

Then he asked what time we wanted to schedule the 45-minute massages included in our weekend package. We had just set foot on the property. We had not even seen the villa. We hadn't begun to plan the next two days. He seemed a bit perturbed.

He looked at his clipboard and asked what time we wanted 'afternoon tea' on the following day. I realized this person was more interested in filling out the form than making us feel welcome.

Now I was perturbed. I told him to take us to our villa right away. We would call him later with answers to his three questions.

Key Learning Point

The staff member's focus was on the clipboard, not the customers. This style of service is tactical, and sometimes practical. It's called **implementation.**

* * *

If the staff was better trained, he might have explained the options in our weekend package like this:

'Breakfast can be served in your room, at the restaurant by the pool, or in the coffee shop overlooking the bay. Room service is open 24 hours. Breakfast buffet at the restaurants is open from 7:00 am to 10:30 am. It's your choice.

'Two 45-minute massages are included in your package,

available anytime from 9:00 am to 10:00 pm. A 90-minute extended massage or 45-minute massage plus optional health treatment is available at an additional charge. A brochure describing the spa and beauty treatments is in your room. Early reservations are recommended.

'Afternoon tea can be delivered to your villa anytime from 2:00 pm – 6:00 pm. The chef likes to prepare it fresh. Just let me know what time is best for you.'

Key Learning Point

This is a higher level of service. Instead of focusing on his questions and his clipboard, the staff works to inform us about our available options. I call this **education.**

* * *

If the staff and the resort were more focused on people than on product, our welcome might have been like this:

'Hello. I'm not sure why you have chosen our resort for the weekend, but whatever your interests, you have come to the right place.

'If you want a weekend of rest and relaxation, room service is available 24 hours for your convenience. We will be glad to serve you breakfast, afternoon tea and any other meals in the privacy of your accommodation.

'In your villa you will find a Jacuzzi and a private pool. Music and videos are also available for your entertainment, just give us a call and we will deliver them to you. If you put up the "Do not disturb" sign, we will only come when you call us for fresh towels, housekeeping or whatever else you may require. You can even have the operator hold all calls. If anyone wishes to contact you, we will slide a note under your door rather than awakening or interrupting you with the phone.

'If you want rest and relaxation, this is the right resort.

'On the other hand, if you want a weekend of activity and

exercise, you have also come to the right place. We have two restaurants overlooking the pool and the bay, a well-equipped workout room, bicycles, two tennis courts and a golf course, a complete water sports facility and a nature trail to hike around the grounds.

'If you want to get out and enjoy an active weekend, you have found the perfect spot.'

Key Learning Point

The resort staff is positive, upbeat and optimistic. His encouragement would make us feel confident about the weekend. Our intentions will be accomplished, desires fulfilled, goals and aspirations will be achieved. This kind of service is **motivation.**

* * *

Now let's go one step higher. What if the staff and resort were committed to truly outstanding service? They would have looked at the guest history and known this was our very first visit. They would have checked the arrival record and seen that we came in from Singapore.

With a warm manner and a genuine smile, the staff in the lobby might have approached us like this:

'Hello, hello and welcome. On behalf of all the staff, thank you for choosing this resort for your weekend away from Singapore. It will be our pleasure to serve you over the next few days. We are truly delighted that you are here.'

Hearing these simple but heartfelt words, we would have sighed deeply and relaxed. A weekend of comfort and care would have begun.

Key Learning Point

This kind of service creates connection with customers as people – beyond products, packages, pricing, policies and procedures. It acknowledges the spirit we share and touches the place in each of us that radiates with loving and light. I call this **inspiration.**

Implementation > Education > Motivation > Inspiration

What level of service do *you* provide?

Is your organization focused on 'getting the job done'? That's implementation.

Are you committed to making your customers 'information rich'? That's education.

Do people feel more able and empowered after speaking with your staff? We're talking motivation.

Are customers uplifted by their interaction with your team? Do they feel better about themselves, their businesses and their future? Now that's inspiration.

Action Steps

The level of service you provide has an impact on your image and your income.

Find out where you are right now and then – *UP Your Service!*

Have you learned to savor the victory?

Making a living usually means generating an income, closing a sale or turning in a profit.

But living a full life also means creating goodwill, opening possibilities and making contributions to others.

Ever found yourself so caught up with 'making a living' that you forget about 'living a life'? Sometimes I do.

Years ago I finished an important corporate event for Singapore Airlines. After the program I immediately debriefed with intense focus on all the things I could have changed, improved or done better.

Mr. Sim Kay Wee, an influential mentor, listened to my long stream of assessments and said, 'You have not learned to savor the victory.' It took me a few years to understand what he said, and a few more to practice what he meant.

Key Learning Point

Life is not just about striving for higher heights; it is also enjoying the steps we take and the friends we make along the way.

Action Steps

Take a moment now to celebrate your life. Harvest your successes and achievements. Whom do you love? Who loves you? What have you accomplished? What have you learned? How have you taken good care of yourself? What generous acts have you done for others? What experiences of partnership, passion and pleasure have you created?

'Perfect lives'

We quest to shape our perfect lives. The right job, the right clothes, the right weight, the right car.

Then nature intervenes. An earthquake can crush that car completely. Floods and tornadoes slash through communities turning houses upside down. How important are the right clothes then?

Your close friend discovers he has a serious medical condition. A close family member struggles with divorce. How important is the right car now?

What does this have to do with you anyway, and why am I writing about it here?

Sometimes perspective is a good thing. Perhaps this page will inspire *you* to do something especially 'nice' for another human being this month.

Write a note to your spouse, children or parents. Give the person sitting next to you a compliment for what they did, or how they look, or just for being 'who they are'.

In the larger scheme of things, it's not so important that we weigh *exactly* the right weight, or wear *just* the right clothes. But it's *very* important that we live, and give, to add a touch of brightness in our remarkably paradoxical world.

More...is more than enough

During the holiday season, and in business generally, we can hear the pursuit of *more*: more money, more customers, more profits, more food, more clothing, more friends, more time, more more.

When is *more*, enough? Do you have enough air to breathe and food to eat? Enough space to live in and business to keep you busy for a while?

If you are reading this now, you've surely got *enough* in your life to give yourself an occasional rest, a break, a moment out of the persistent quest for *more*...a chance to really enjoy what you already have, which most of the time is quite enough.

This is not a call to discard ambition or quell your quest for greater goals. Rather, this is an invitation to enjoy a moment of relaxation where you are, calm in all that is, comfortable in all you have, and grateful for the chance just to be here.

That's enough.

UP Your Service! learning resources

Complete active learning systems to improve your service and get your customers' loyalty going UP! Ron Kaufman's best teaching and stories in studio-quality video and audio. Easy-to-use. Proven effective worldwide. *Backed by Ron's 100%, no-risk, money-back guarantee.* Order now. Details on page 247, or visit www.UpYourService.com

The Secrets of Superior Service

Eight steps to achieve superior service:
- Fly over rising expectations
  - Excellent service mindset
  - Improving service standards
  - Managing customer expectations
  - Bounce back with service recovery
  - Appreciate complaining customers
  - Take personal responsibility
  - See the world from your
    customer's point of view.

High-impact training for everyone in the organization. Three hours of engaging video and audio, with mini-posters of key learning points, discussion guide and workbook.

S$388 (US$288) ISBN 981-00-8946-5

Partnership Power*!*

How to build positive, progressive, proactive partnerships both inside and outside your organization. Excellent for deepening relationships with customers and suppliers, colleagues, distributors and other partners. Best practice examples in the essential service cycle of *explore, agree, deliver, assure.* These principles work in your personal life, too! Three intensive hours on video and audio, plus viewer's guide with key learning points.

S$388 (US$288) ISBN 981-04-1787-X

Service Encounters of the Third Kind

Shift your focus from mere 'transaction satisfaction' to creating profitable, long-term 'customer loyalty'. Learn the shifts you and your team must make in training, mindset, focus and goals. And make them!

Essential education for service supervisors and management teams. The future is determined by the actions you take today. This shows you exactly what to do! One hour on video and audio with viewer's guide.

S$288 (US$218) ISBN 981-00-8948-1

Quality Service – LIVE!

One of Ron's hottest presentations with a LIVE audience of 3,000 enthusiastic fans. World-class *education* and *motivation* in a one-hour video. Get your team pumped up and ready to *serve*. Terrific for staff meetings and fast training programs.

S$59 (US$39) ISBN 981-04-1661-X (VHS)
S$59 (US$39) ISBN 981-04-6228-X (VCD)

Ron Kaufman is *Unbelievable!*

Break through the glass ceiling to reach the *top* and achieve your highest goals. Profit from this LIVE inspirational speech for an audience of 2,000 insurance agents in Singapore. Tailored for the industry and the local audience. One hour of fast-action ideas, insights and humor.

S$59 (US$39) ISBN 981-00-8949-X

Your absolutely no-risk, money-back guarantee
Your investment in these active learning programs is *100% guaranteed.* Use them for 90 days. If you are not completely satisfied with the impact on your people and your service, return for a complete refund.

UP Your Service! - #1 Bestseller!

Strategies and Action Steps to Delight Your Customers NOW!

Sharing this book is one sure way to *UP Your Service!* – and improve the service you get from others. Give copies to all your colleagues, customers, suppliers, family members and other important partners in your life.

320 pages, 137 illustrations
S$25 (US$18) ISBN 981-04-2132-X

'Ron Kaufman is a practical philosopher of customer service. He gives you a map you can follow with your head and your heart. Ron's practical strategies show how to generate superb service as an individual, a team or a company. The name of the game today is inspirational service. Ron Kaufman can help us all win.'

Philip Hallstein
Executive Vice President, **SportsMind**

UP Your Service! INSIGHTS

Get absolutely inspired with amazing stories of spectacular service – and how you can do it, too. Real drama and trauma of service disasters – and what you must avoid. Key lessons and learning points to motivate your staff, align your team, build your service culture, and keep your customers coming back for more.

Join Ron Kaufman on an incredible trip around the world in the quest for superior service.

268 pages, 174 illustrations
S$25 (US$18) ISBN 981-04-5939-4

Books make terrific training tools and motivating gifts. Special rates are available for volume orders. For details, send an e-mail message to Orders@RonKaufman.com

Free monthly newsletter by e-mail

Now you can receive Ron Kaufman's free monthly newsletter, *The Best of Active Learning*. It's packed with real stories and practical ideas – key learning points and action steps to boost your service, partnerships and culture. To get your free subscription, send an e-mail message to:

join-bestof@RonKaufman.com

If you wish to subscribe a team or workgroup, please seek their agreement in advance. Then send a list of e-mail addresses in the body of your message and we will subscribe them for you.

Best of Active Learning

Now available in audio – 53 of Ron's best newsletter stories and ideas. Real examples of spectacular service, legendary team-work and winning company cultures. Learn from benchmark companies around the world including Citibank, Disneyland, Federal Express, Hewlett Packard, IBM, Singapore Airlines and many others. More than two hours on three full-length cassettes.

S$49 (US$35) ISBN 981-04-1663-6

To place your order now:

1. Order **on-line:**   www.RonKaufman.com/
                         products.html

2. Order by **e-mail:** Orders@RonKaufman.com

2. Order by **fax:**   (+65) 6444-8292

3. Order by **mail:**   Ron Kaufman Pte Ltd
                         50 Bayshore Park #31-01
                         Aquamarine Tower
                         Singapore 469977

When ordering, please include your selections, name, address, fax, telephone, e-mail and credit card information. Credit cards are charged in Singapore dollars. Deliveries by courier at cost. For videotape, indicate preference for PAL or NTSC format.